Motorbooks International Illustrated Buyer's Guide Series

Illustrated

# INTERNATIONAL HARVESTER TRACTOR

## BUYER'S ★ GUIDE

Robert N. Pripps

Motorbooks International
Publishers & Wholesalers

*To my granddaughters, Jessica, Hannah, and Leah Pripps*

First published in 1995 by Motorbooks International Publishers & Wholesalers, PO Box 2, 729 Prospect Avenue, Osceola, WI 54020 USA

Motorbooks International books are also available at discounts in bulk quantity for industrial or sales-promotional use. For details write to Special Sales Manager at the Publisher's address

Library of Congress Cataloging-in-Publication Data
Pripps, Robert N.
    Illustrated International Harvester tractor buyer's guide/Robert N. Pripps.
        p. cm. —(Motorbooks International illustrated buyer's guide series)
    Includes index.
    ISBN 0-7603-0011-9
    1. IHC tractors—Purchasing. 2. IHC tractors —History.
I. Title. II. Series.
TL233.5.P758     1995
629.225—dc20                 94-44212

*On the front cover:* Norm Seveik of Northfield, Minnesota, owns this beautiful 1940 McCormick Farmall wide-front Model A tractor. *Andrew Morland*

*On the back cover:* (top) the Farmall F-12 was a 15hp tractor introduced in 1932. It was available in either gasoline or kerosene versions and used a three-speed transmission; (middle) the McCormick-Deering W-30 was a standard-tread version of the Farmall F-30. The W-30 was built between 1932 and 1940 and used as an industrial tractor; (bottom) a 1939 Farmall H, owned by Brett Shoger, shown at the 1994 Sandwich, Illinois, show. Even after fifty-five years, it looks quite modern.

Printed and bound in the United States of America

# Contents

# Foreword

This book covers a forty-year period of the history of the world's greatest farm implement maker: International Harvester. During these years, from 1921 to 1961, Harvester made some of the world's greatest tractors. Although these machines were made by the hundreds of thousands, certain models and styles have become much sought-after collectors' items. It is the purpose of this book to classify all the IH tractors from this period according to their collectability.

These tractors have been classified primarily on the basis of model numbers, type, or style produced. Some weight is also given to age.

The book covers only wheel tractors and not the great IH crawlers. This was done simply to limit the scope. The way crawler tractor collecting is catching on, a crawler buyer's guide should be available soon.

---

# Acknowledgments

I am extremely appreciative of the help given to me by the dedicated collectors whose International tractors appear in this book. I thank Mr. C.H. Wendel; if it hadn't been for his great book, *150 Years of International Harvester*, I'm not sure I would have sorted out all the different IH models. Special thanks go to Harvester collector Ralph Johnson, of Waterman, Illinois, who graciously consented to review the manuscript and the collectability ratings; and to Michael Dregni, Editor in Chief, and his staff at Motorbooks International. This *International Harvester Tractor Buyer's Guide* was Michael's idea.

# Introduction and Investment Rating

A star rating system is becoming standard among antique collectors to indicate investment potential at a glance. For collector tractors, the rating does not have to do with the condition of the machine but with its uniqueness and desirability as indicated below:

★★★★★ Five Stars: the best investment. To be given a five-star rating a tractor must be historically significant. That is, it should be the first or last of a production sequence, an experimental model, a model with a limited production run, or a model that (because of age or attrition) has become unique. A five-star rating assumes an impeccable restoration, but even if not restored, the investment potential is there. These tractors are rare and expensive (unless the present owner is unaware of what he or she has). Because of this rarity, continued appreciation can be expected and should far outstrip inflation. Most often the existence and location of five-star tractors are known by the major collectors. These are sold or traded without the general public or lesser collectors being aware of their availability.

★★★★ Four Stars: excellent investment potential. Four-star rated tractors are still quite expensive, but appreciation should continue to exceed inflation. To be given a four-star rating tractors must meet the same requirements as the five-star tractors, but to a lesser extent. The break between four and five stars is open to interpretation and is, of course, subjective. The same is true of the lower ratings.

★★★ Three Stars: very good investments if ownership satisfaction is considered. These are less expensive to buy than four- or five-star-rated tractors, and they will appreciate at a lower rate. Inflation will just about equal appreciation on a three-star tractor. These represent the best compromise between desirability and cost.

★★ Two Stars: good investments, but with the cost of ownership. These are tractors that are too new or were produced in such numbers that they have not yet developed an appreciation history.

★ One Star: marginal investments. These are tractors so new, or so common, or that have been modified to such an extent that they have no antique value. Also in this category are two-star tractors built without equipment, such as hydraulics or electrical systems, that were generally available for the type, and tractors with such bad reputations that they have no nostalgic value. Bear in mind that such reputations fade with time and, as the majority of one-star machines get scrapped, the remainder move up in the star ratings. One-star tractors are for those who have storage space and are in it for the long haul.

### How to Use the Star Ratings

At the beginning of each chapter is a star rating chart. The basic star rating of each model is given. In the following chapters, additional stars are awarded for variations on the basic theme, such as high-crop models and so on. In addition, another star should be given for tractors with serial numbers in the first or last 10 percent of a model's run, unless they already have five stars.

As tractor collecting becomes increasingly popular, perfection is being achieved by more and more collectors in their restoration efforts. To set their tractors off from similar restorations, collectors are obtaining and

This farm magazine ad from 1936 highlights the complete line of McCormick-Deering tractors from the W-12 to the WD-40.

restoring appropriate implements to show with their tractors, the more unusual the better. Front-mounted implements, such as cultivators and loaders are to be avoided, however, as they obscure the lines of the tractor itself.

This book portrays, in word and picture, forty years of International Harvester tractors. Not the first forty years, to be sure, as Harvester had been building tractors for fifteen years by 1921, when our account begins. Quite a number of tractors from this earlier period are in the hands of collectors. All are in the four- or five-star category, and a guidebook is of little use.

During the years between 1921 to 1961 tractors by International Harvester had a profound impact on the agricultural industry of the world. They were trend-setters. They reflected the strong heritage of the McCormicks and Deerings and their commitment to quality and product support. These families took seriously the fact that their names were on the products.

Tractors from this forty-year period are the ones most Harvester collectors are interested in. My purpose in writing this book is to encourage and assist the collector in understanding the International Harvester line of tractors and how they came to be the way they are. I also want to assure Harvester tractor collectors of the historic value of their machines.

Certainly, my opinions of the investment ratings of these great old tractors are subjective. For comments and corrections, write to me in care of the publisher.

*Robert N. Pripps*

# Chapter 1

# Family History

*Let us not forget that cultivation of
the earth is the most important labor of man.*
Daniel Webster

## A Time for Invention

Necessity is generally considered to be the mother of invention, but this was not the case with the reaping machine. One might say that the reaping machine was the mother of all inventions, at least as far as farming is concerned.

Since the days of Adam and Eve, farmers had scratched out their living with rudimentary tools. Each farmer could till and harvest an acre or two, growing food for his own family. Then came feudalism, and with it, a small amount of specialization. Farmers no longer grew food for just their own families. They also provided for a new nonfarming community, which included, among others, the lords and nobles, their servants, and soldiers. As late as 1830, three-quarters of the U.S. population of thirteen million lived on farms, but as the world's population grew, more nonfarm people depended on the farmer for food. The farmer, his family, and his hired hands were proving that they could grow enough food to fill the country's demand, and at a reasonable price.

The work was tiring, disheartening, and even degrading. Until the invention of the cradle-scythe, the stoop-labor of wielding the sickle kept a man's head bowed. Threshing and winnowing were inefficient and time consuming. Generally the farm animals fared better than the humans.

The world was ready for the reaper in 1831, even though it did not know it. With the successful reaper came the necessity for the threshing machine. Also, since a man could now harvest forty acres, he had to have a means of tilling forty acres. Thus the steel or chilled cast iron plow became an essential tool.

Steel for these new tools would not have been available in the quantities needed or at the prices required if it had not been for Sir Henry Bessemer and his steel-making process. Now that steel was available for rails and boilers, steam engines facilitated necessary transportation.

Vast industries sprang up peopled by farm workers displaced by the new machinery. Thus, in the seventy years following the invention of the reaper, more than half of the U.S. population of sixty-three million became city dwellers.

## The Reaper

It is doubtful that Cyrus Hall McCormick knew what an earth-shaking event was taking place on a hot July afternoon in 1831 in Walnut Grove, Virginia. His reaping machine, pulled by a single horse, advanced through the grain. Old Jo Anderson, McCormick's slave, walked beside the machine, raking off the severed stalks from the platform into bundles ready for binding. McCormick himself

E.A. Johnston, one of the geniuses behind International Harvester tractors. Johnston acquired 162 patents for IH during his forty years with the firm. Besides being credited with the rear power take-off and the PTO binder, Johnston was instrumental in the development of the Farmall.

paced after the reaper, oblivious to the crowd that was gathering. Most likely, his thoughts were not of great industry but of using the machine for his own harvest.

Cyrus was born to Robert and Mary Ann Hall-McCormick on February 15, 1809. Robert McCormick, Cyrus's Scottish/Irish father, was a wealthy Virginia land-baron, with more than five hundred acres of land. His estate had its own grist mill, sawmill, smelter, distillery, and blacksmith shop. Robert McCormick was an imaginative man with mechanical ingenuity. He tinkered with the invention of a mechanical reaper as early as 1809, but success was to wait for his son Cyrus Hall McCormick. Robert succeeded in making a grain cutter, but it left the grain stalks too tangled for binding.

Cyrus was party to these endeavors as he grew up. He started his efforts soon after his father returned his final unsuccessful machine to the shed. Capitalizing on his father's experiences, he built some working models. Because communications were so imperfect in those days, McCormick was unaware of the efforts of others who were working on similar machines at the time.

After modifying his model several times, McCormick came up with a machine with a straight serrated cutter bar with fingers, driven by the single wheel. A platform extended sideways from the wheel. A divider was installed on the outboard end of the cutter to separate the grain to be cut from that to be left for the next round. A large reel, also rotated by the wheel, guided the grain to be cut into the cutter bar. Two men and a horse with a McCormick reaper could harvest about an acre per hour.

McCormick sold a few reapers along the lines of his first model. Nevertheless, farmers did not clamor for them, and for the most part, considered them curiosities. Farms of the 1830s in America were not sufficiently developed to be free of stumps, humps, and rocks. Farmers were skeptical of the machine's ability to work under these conditions. McCormick also encountered resentment by farm laborers who thought that these machines would throw them out of work.

Besides the lack of a market for reapers, Cyrus McCormick and his father had their interests diverted to other pursuits at the time, including other farm inventions and manufacturing activities. One such diversion was the McCormick cast iron plow, which sold very well in the period before the steel plow was invented. But while their attention was elsewhere, Obed Hussey secured the first U.S. patent for a reaping machine in 1833.

The Hussey patent got Cyrus's attention back to reapers. He immediately filed for his own patent, which was granted in 1834. Thus began a bitter conflict that lasted for years.

Hussey's reaper was somewhat different from McCormick's in that it had two drive wheels, plus smaller wheels to carry the cutter; it used no reel, nor was side delivery provided. Thus the binder had to keep up with the machine in order for the sheaves to be out of the way before it came around again. The main advantage of the Hussey reaper was the open-top guard finger bar that allowed chaff and other debris to exit, instead of plugging up and jamming the cutter.

## The McCormick Harvesting Machine Company

By 1840, McCormick entered the marketplace in earnest. Due to some unfortunate changes, the Hussey machine's popularity began to wane. Hussey challenged McCormick to a field trial. By 1843 Hussey and McCormick agreed to the public contest, which was to be held in the James River area of Virginia. Each machine was to harvest similar plots of the same field. The first one done was the winner. In two events, McCormick's reaper finished ahead of Hussey's. Hussey continued to challenge McCormick in the field and in the courtroom until his death in 1860 in a railroad accident. Unfortunately for both men, their patents expired just about the time that mechanical reaping was gaining wide acceptance with the farmers. Mechanical reaping really caught on when the self-raker came on the market. Later, self-tying binders made all the old reapers obsolete.

In the winter of 1844, C.H. McCormick took a trip west to see about selling reapers in Wisconsin, Illinois, and Ohio. When he saw the broad, flat fields he remarked that reapers were a luxury in Virginia but a necessity here. McCormick realized that central Virginia would never do as a center from which to distribute reaping machines to the plains states of the West.

McCormick first sold manufacturing rights to Seymour and Morgan, in Brockport, New York. Next he dispatched brother Leander, now twenty-eight years old, to Cincinnati to make a similar arrangement there. More than one hundred reapers per year were sold from these two locations and the Virginia facilities, and McCormick garnered royalties on those sold by the others. As the patent protection neared its fourteen-year end, Seymour and Morgan began to advocate the denial of an extension, because of the monopoly by McCormick and because the royalties he charged hurt the farmers. Seymour and Morgan had particular political clout and so prevailed. Mc-

Cyrus Hall (C.H.) McCormick, born in 1809, lived to see the great transformation in mechanized agriculture. McCormick was forty years old before he realized much success from his invention of a reaping machine. He was a tall man with a determined personality that engendered fierce loyalty from his employees. At age forty-eight, McCormick married Nancy Fowler. Among their descendants were Cyrus Hall McCormick Jr. and Cyrus Hall McCormick III, both instrumental in guiding the great empire created by C.H. McCormick. After her husband's death in 1884, Nancy McCormick was the principle owner of International Harvester; a woman running a large business was a rarity in those days.

Cormick was then without patent coverage on his basic ideas.

In 1847, thirty-eight-year-old McCormick moved to Chicago with $60 in his pockets. Through drive and ability he was a millionaire before his fortieth birthday. Chicago was only a town of 17,000 people at the time. The land was mostly swamp and required drainage before it could be used, but it was cheap. Chicago was the center of opportunity for the West.

In Chicago, McCormick entered into a partnership with one C.M. Gray. While McCormick was away from Chicago, Gray sold half of his half interest in the new company to

The ultimate in International Harvester tractors are the big articulated four-wheel drive models with their control centers located behind the articulation point. This one is seen at the 1994 Waukee, Iowa, show.

Messrs. Ogden and Jones. Needless to say, McCormick was upset over the arrangement and took Gray to court. While the matter was awaiting decision, Gray sold the remaining portion of his interest to Ogden. Thus, in 1848, the business was renamed McCormick, Ogden and Company, with Jones still a junior partner. By September of the next year, Ogden and Jones sold their interests to McCormick for $65,000. In 1849, despite the severe competition resulting from the loss of patent protection, 1,500 reapers were sold by McCormick.

Severe competition continued as each of the thirty concerns that had copied the basic reaper tried to be first to acquire the manufacturing rights to promising new inventions. Each competitor had machinery agents scour-

ing rural America searching for customers to fight over, with the salesmen sometimes coming to blows.

To help him run his burgeoning business, Cyrus invited his brothers, Leander and William, to come to Chicago to help him. Things went well until William died in 1865, and disagreement arose over the distribution of his estate. Cyrus and Leander did not get along well from then on. In 1879, the partnership was changed into a corporation, with Cyrus holding three-fourths of the stock and Leander the balance.

Cyrus H. McCormick died in 1884 after witnessing the great revolution in mechanized agriculture, after acquiring great wealth, and after seeing his reaper company grow to become the largest of its kind. His widow, Nancy Fowler McCormick, and son, Cyrus Jr., bought out Leander's interest in 1890. By this time, however, McCormick's preeminence in the field was being seriously challenged. This was due primarily to McCormick's slowness in picking up promising new invention rights, and a result, for the most part, of the bickering between the brothers.

## Deering Harvester Company

William Deering was one of those who capitalized on McCormick's slowness. McCormick had been in the reaper business for about forty years when Deering, then forty-four years old, bought into the rights to the Marsh Harvester, an up-and-coming competitor to McCormick.

Prior to entering the implement business, William Deering had made a substantial fortune in the wholesale dry goods business in the state of Maine. In 1870, he made his way to Chicago to make some land investments, and called on an acquaintance named Elijah Gammon. Gammon was a retired Methodist preacher, who had become a partner in the firm that was attempting to manufacture the Marsh Harvester. Gammon persuaded Deering to look no further for investments, and to put his money into the Harvester company. Two years later, when the books showed that Deering had doubled his money, he asked to be taken into the business as a partner. By the next year, poor health caused Gammon to call for Deering to move to Chicago and take over management of the business. In 1880, Gammon sold out to Deering who, up until that time, had no experience in agriculture.

Prior to 1880, the reaper had been modified into the wire-tie binder. The sheaves of grain were now bound while still on board the machine by means of a fine wire wrapped around them and twisted. While this saved much in labor costs, there was the problem of animals eating broken wires, and also, the bundles had to be unbound for threshing. While the McCormicks bickered, Deering bought the rights to the invention of John Appleby, which substituted twine for wire, thus solving both problems associated with the wire-tie binder.

In 1880, Deering sold more than 3,000 twine binders, and the days of the wire-tie were over. In one year Deering had built a new Chicago factory, bought an untried patent, built it into a successful machine and captured the lion's share of an industry already crowded with experienced competitors.

The idea of amalgamation, wrote Cyrus Hall McCormick III, was first broached between C.H. McCormick and Deering before the former's death in 1884. Nothing came of it, however, because the tempers of those first-generation harvester men were too individualistic. After the death of C.H. McCormick, the records are full of accounts of meetings called to consider a merger including smaller implement companies. The smaller companies recognized that the present competitive atmosphere would be ruinous for all concerned and wanted, at the very least, an understanding on pricing.

## The American Harvester Company

By 1890, McCormick and Deering were the commanding leaders in the harvesting industry. Deering, by now getting on in years, encouraged consolidation. In the fall of 1890, the McCormick Harvesting Machine Company, the Deering Harvester Company, and eighteen other competitors met in Chicago to attempt the industry's first amalgamation. An industrial giant emerged, dubbed the American Harvester Company. The six chief shareholders became directors of the new corporation, with Cyrus McCormick Jr. as president and the aging Deering as chairman.

However, the American Harvester Company was doomed from the start. At the time of the merger, all of the harvesting companies bought their knives and cutters from the Whitman, Barnes Company, in Akron, Ohio. Its president, Colonel A.L. Conger, conceived the idea for the American Harvester Company in which his own little concern would be preserved. In the several years before the grand Chicago merger meeting, Colonel Conger talked up the idea with all his customers as he made the rounds on selling trips. His mistake was in encouraging each of the smaller entrepreneurs to establish their own company value, without benefit of formal appraisal.

The latest of the large and small from Case International were shown at the 1994 Sandwich, Illinois, show by dealers Leffelman and Sons of Amboy, Illinois. The marriage of the two rival tractor companies was as troubling to some as the original wedding of McCormick and Deering. Bad economic times in the sixties, plus some unfortunate management decisions set Harvester up for a disastrous six-month labor strike. The conglomerate Tenneco had just picked up a foundering Case Company and reasoned correctly that folding them together with International would have synergistic results.

These were the values attributed to each company when the consolidation occurred. While the valuation of the new company was high, banks saw through the scheme and refused to lend working capital. McCormick and Deering balked at supplying the funding for what they saw as weaker competitors, and so the short-lived American Harvester Company foundered. The government also was threatening involvement under the newly passed Sherman Antitrust Act, as the consolidation was seen as restraint of trade.

For the next decade, the industry vacillated between merger and ruinous competition. Deering proposed, in 1897, to sell out to Cyrus McCormick Jr., but McCormick was unable to raise the cash. Vigorous competition resumed, with Deering continuing to gain on McCormick's leadership.

Twice more the two giants of the harvester industry tried to arrange an end to their disastrous competition. Twice more they failed to reach agreement. Each time they failed, competition resumed with an even more intense vigor.

*Right*
This December 1928 McCormick-Deering ad is rich with the romance of winter time farm life. Note the phrase, "As you sit by the fire, take stock of your equipment and power."

## The McCormick-Deering Line *of* Farm-Operating Equipment

Grain Binders
Rice Binders
Push Binders & Headers
Reapers
Harvester-Threshers
Threshers
Rice Threshers
Alfalfa Threshers
Mowers
Side Rakes & Tedders
Dump Rakes
Sweep Rakes
Tedders
Hay Loaders
Stackers
Baling Presses
Corn Planters
Cotton Planters
Listers
Drills
Cultivators
Huskers & Shredders
Corn Binders
Ensilage Cutters
Ensilage Harvesters
Ensilage Blowers
Corn Pickers
Corn Shellers
Grain Drills
Broadcast Seeders
Alfalfa & Grass Drills
Lime Sowers
Fertilizer Distributors
Potato Planters
Potato Diggers
Disk Harrows
Peg-tooth Harrows
Spring-tooth Harrows
One-horse Cultivators
Orchard Cultivators
Field Cultivators
Rod Weeders
Rotary Hoes
10-20 Tractors
15-30 Tractors
Industrial Tractors
Farmall Tractors
Farmall Machines
Tractor Plows
Horse Plows
Harrow Plows
Ridge Busters
Soil Pulverizers
Beet Seeders
Beet Cultivators
Beet Pullers
Motor Trucks
Motor Coaches
Engines
Wagons & Trucks
Cream Separators
Manure Spreaders
Stalk Cutters
Stubble Pulverizers
Feed Grinders
Knife Grinders
Cane Mills, etc.
Repairs
Twine

Founded on the McCormick reaper invented in 1831. Sold and serviced by the McCormick-Deering dealers in 15,000 communities.

# Winter Is a Time *for* Planning

THE NEW YEAR lies ahead. Snow glistens like a blanket on the fields, and underneath lie the secrets of next summer's harvests. In the spring Nature will wake the life in the soil, but man will *direct* it.

The American farmer is always improving the things he has done. He goes on compounding farm science and knowledge, motive power and mechanical equipment. The more he works with his brains, intelligently, the less he toils with his hands. His own muscle power is as limited as it was in Adam's time and the hand work of his hired hands is very, very costly. He puts the burden onto machines—*broad-capacity, fast-working, cost-reducing, profit-making equipment and power.* He is abreast with the best of men and he competes with the world. *He forces the issue in farming and profit comes his way.*

\*　　\*　　\*　　\*

THERE is plenty of work for winter on the farm but there is also time for leisure, and for enjoyment of the many good things our civilization provides. And for planning, too. As you sit by the fire, take stock of your equipment and power. Changes have been coming fast of late years. Labor-saving methods and machines are giving wonderful advantages into the hands of the forward-looking farmer—advantages of *capacity* and *profit.* The old reliable McCormick-Deering lines are listed here for your convenience, *and among them are many recent developments.* More than ever it is a certainty that "Good Equipment Makes a Good Farmer Better."

### INTERNATIONAL HARVESTER COMPANY

506 So. Michigan Ave.  of America *(Incorporated)*  Chicago, Ill.

# McCormick-Deering

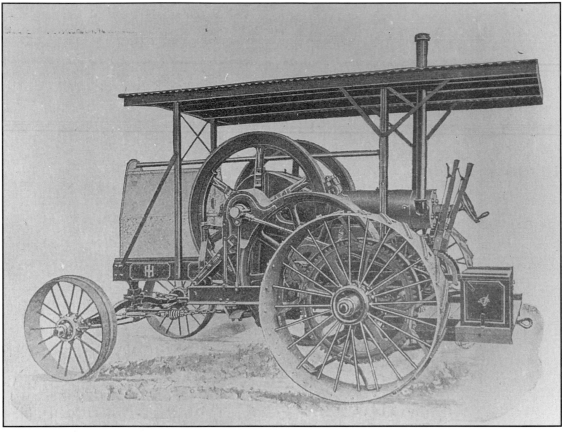

A 1908 version of the Type A friction-drive tractor by International Harvester. Harvester's first tractor came out in 1906. All were assembled at the Upper Sandusky, Ohio, plant, using engines shipped from the Milwaukee plant.

## The International Harvester Company

The years 1896 and 1897 saw a severe recession in American business. This was due in large extent to saturation of markets through devastating price wars. Companies reacted by merging to eliminate competition as the economy recovered from the recession. Between 1898 and 1902, 212 consolidations occurred, almost twice the number occurring in the preceding nine years.

In June 1902, Cyrus Hall McCormick Jr., the son of the late inventor, made a trip to New York to see about arranging financing through the J.P. Morgan Company. McCormick met with a junior partner, George W. Perkins. Perkins assured McCormick that financing was available, but then began asking questions about the harvester business and the companies involved. Before McCormick left that day, Perkins asked if he would be interested in merging his company into a larger conglomerate, with McCormick predominant. McCormick said he was interested.

Over the next two hot New York months, negotiators from McCormick, Deering, the Plano Harvester of Chicago, Warder, Bushnell & Glessner of Springfield, Ohio, and Milwaukee Harvester Company of Milwaukee, Wisconsin, lived in hotel suites receiving calls from Perkins. The banker went from one group to the other pointing out the advantages of merger and handling objections. Over time, Perkins won the confidence of the machinery men from the Midwest, and finally, in

The Mogul Jr. was a single-cylinder version of the behemoth Mogul 30-60. Introduced in 1911, it weighed little over 15,000lb. McCormick dealers sold the Mogul line of tractors.

The Mogul 10-20 was an early attempt by Mc-Cormick to get the size of its tractors down. This one is configured for one-man operation with a binder.

late July, got them all around the same table. On August 12, they agreed to become the International Harvester Company.

George W. Perkins proposed a ten-year stock trust. The trust would hold all the stock of the new International Harvester Company, with Perkins, McCormick, and Charles Deering (William's son) serving as trustees.

Thus, after more than ten years of cat-and-mouse, International Harvester Company was born. The name, picked by George Perkins, was selected to reflect its global scope. Harvester, as it came to be called, controlled 85 percent of U.S. harvester production and boasted assets of $110 million (a staggering amount in 1902). Included were malleable iron works, twine factories, timberlands and sawmills, hemp properties, coal and iron mines, and the Illinois Northern Railway, plus the plants in Chicago, Milwaukee, and Ohio.

The stockholders of the new concern had every reason to be confident, and they were

not disappointed. Although profit margins were small at first, the company's monopolistic position, its reputation for producing good equipment, and its strong dealer network assured success. There were still many serious internal struggles, however. It was fortunate that Perkins, representing the Morgan financial interests, was able to override the petty squabbles between the McCormick and the Deering factions. He became fed up with Harvester's "millionaire officers" who refused to work or follow orders. He was finally able to promote Clarence Funk, a capable professional executive with ties to neither family, to General Manager.

After expiration of the voting trust set up by Perkins, the McCormicks borrowed $5 million from John D. Rockefeller to regain control. Rather than reinstate their own rather inept family management, the McCormicks stuck with Perkins' idea of professional management. Their first move after regaining control was to fire Funk, who was a decent professional manager, but not particularly loyal to the McCormicks. He was replaced by Alexander Legge, a McCormick loyalist. The talented Legge, who had worked himself up from a position in a field office collecting bad debts from farmers, was one of the key players in the events that followed.

## The Early Tractor Years

The new International Harvester Company had acquired thriving businesses, with factories, staff, and established positions in the market. One of these, the Milwaukee Company, was producing a line of large stationary gasoline engines. Another plant, in Upper Sandusky, Ohio, built truck parts. International Harvester's first tractor was assembled in 1906 in the Upper Sandusky plant, using an engine shipped down from Milwaukee. The engine was a single cylinder four-cycle unit of 15hp. It had an open crankcase, make-break ignition, and spray tank water cooling. A friction drive connected the engine output to the wheels. The whole power plant was shifted on rollers to engage the friction drive.

Twenty-five of these large machines were built and sent into the field for testing. The following year, two hundred more were built. It soon became apparent that the friction drive was not adequate. In 1908, production was transferred to the Milwaukee plant, and a gear drive was substituted. Three sizes were built: 15, 20, and 40hp.

At this time, Canada, with its vast prairie farms, was the leading tractor market. In the summer of 1908, the first of the Winnipeg tractor trials was held. Six gasoline and five steam tractors competed. Three of the six gasoline tractors were from International

The Titan 10-20 looked much the same as the Mogul. Titan tractors were sold by Deering dealers; between 1916 and 1922, some 78,000 Titan 10-20s were delivered. The Titan was a two-cylinder, however, while the Mogul had one.

Harvester. A Kinnard-Haines gasoline tractor won the event with 117.6 points out of a possible 155. The 15hp Harvester model came in second with 117 points. The success of these gasoline tractors spelled the doom of the steam engine. The perfection of kerosene as a tractor fuel further sealed the demise of steam by eliminating the high cost of burning gasoline.

The Canadians dictated the tractor market. They wanted large tractors for their farms, which stretched from horizon to horizon. They wanted a tractor that could pull as many as fifteen plow bottoms, inching its way across the prairie. By 1910, International Harvester's largest tractor produced 45hp. It weighed over 20,000lb.

The year 1910 also saw tractor production at the Chicago Tractor Works. The new design was called the Mogul. It had a 45hp two-cylinder four-cycle horizontally opposed engine. It had spur gears for forward motion but used a friction reverse.

Threshermen railed against internal combustion, but at the 1910 Winnipeg Trials, when Rumely deserted the ranks of steam and entered "Kerosene Annie," the threshermen began to come around. Harvester surpassed Hart-Parr that same year in the number of tractors produced. Also, in 1911, Harvester joined the ranks of those producing kerosene tractors when they added the 45hp Titan to their line.

At this point in history, International Harvester still had separate dealerships for McCormick and Deering lines of products. The Mogul tractors were made for McCormick dealers while the Titan was sold by Deering

The Titan 10-20 relied on a large water tank for cooling its two-cylinder engine. Water circulated by gravity: no water pump, fan, or radiator was used.

dealers. By 1911, the Mogul was upgraded with a larger engine to the 30 to 60hp class. The Titan was also upgraded before the end of the year to the same power class. The Titan used an entirely different engine, however. It had two cylinders, but they were side-by-side. The pistons operated in unison, providing an even distribution of power pulses, but requiring massive flywheels.

The Canadians were still driving the market toward ever larger machines while the editors of U.S. farm magazines clamored for smaller tractors for the U.S. market, and, indeed, the market for much of the world.

The call for smaller tractors was aided in 1914 by a poor harvest. This was also the year that World War I broke out in Europe. These two factors caused a collapse of the land boom in western Canada, and with the latter, a col-lapse of the large tractor market. Despite making excellent tractors and threshers, the Rumely organization also collapsed that year. Harvester's fortunes were at a low ebb, as well, having at that time its worst credit ratio in its history.

In 1913 an outfit called the Bull Tractor Company had introduced a 12hp, single-wheel-drive tractor selling for around $400. This trim, agile little device rattled the industry as it out-maneuvered the doddering behemoths it competed against. While it was never a mechanically sound concept, it did sweep the field of customers, and in 1914 was first in sales, thereby displacing International Harvester. Its popularity did not last long, but it did spawn a subsidiary much in evidence today: Toro, the lawn, garden, and golf course equipment maker.

A 1913 45hp Titan, owned by the American Thresherman's Association, is shown at the 1992 Midwest Thresherman's Reunion in Pontiac, Illinois.

As smaller, lighter tractors made the scene, an additional benefit was realized by the farmer: he could convert his horse-drawn implements to tractor use, thereby saving considerably on cost. Many of these implements did not fully utilize the tractor's capability, and others were simply not strong enough to stand up, but the transition to power farming was being made.

The rapid rise of the automobile also affected the tractor industry as advances brought by large production trickled down. There were ten times as many automobiles in use in 1925 as there were in 1910, and as farmers availed themselves of the benefits of the automobile, they also became more comfortable with the tractor, especially a smaller tractor that had features and controls similar to the car.

Persistent borrowing of automobile technology indicated to many that the tractor had more in common with the automobile than with implements such as plows and threshers. Therefore, it was not a great step of faith to believe rumors as early as 1914 that Henry Ford was about to get into the tractor business. Ford had been experimenting with "automobile plows" as early as 1906. One effect of the Ford rumors was that a group of Minneapolis entrepreneurs, which included a man by the name of Ford, organized The Ford Tractor Company, attempting to capitalize on the magic name. Although this outfit did actually make and sell a few tractors, their efforts, like their tractors, were short-lived.

The Minneapolis Ford tractor had less of an impact on power farming than did a spate of Ford Model T car-to-tractor conversion kits that came out at about that time. C.H. Wendel lists forty-five kit manufacturers, as of 1919, in his book *Encyclopedia of American Farm Tractors*. These kits, which were advertised as being easy to install and remove, usually included large lugged wheels to be mounted on a frame extension with chain reduction drives from the regular axles. Costing around $200, these kits did fill the bill for many a two- or three-horse farmer, but their usefulness was definitely limited. However, the Model T itself did quite well under these trying circumstances, further endearing it to the hapless small farmer. Henry Ford must have relished the publicity garnered for his Model T and in no way discouraged the kitmakers.

International Harvester was quick to get into the small tractor fray with their single-cylinder, chain-drive Mogul 8-16 and their two-cylinder, two-speed, chain-drive Titan 10-20. Some friction began between the dealerships, however, because in designing the Titan after the Mogul, the engineers used the experiences of the first to make improvements in the second. Also, the Titan was a three-plow machine, while the Mogul was only rated for two. Therefore, the Mogul 8-16 was revised and modernized for the next year to the 10-20. For several years they simultaneously built the Mogul 10-20, the Titan 10-20, and the International 8-16. The International 8-16 used the four-cylinder engine, hood, and radiator of the International truck, which was then being built in the Springfield, Ohio, plant.

By 1915, the slump in tractor demand was over. Wartime food demands put even more of the Great Plains of the United States and Canada under the plow. In 1917, about 25 percent of U.S. tractor production was sent overseas. International Harvester was the world's leading tractor producer, followed by Case, Avery, and Moline.

### Harvester's Legal Battle

After its formation in 1902, International Harvester had been under almost continuous legal attack by individual state governments. In 1912, things got immeasurably worse for Harvester when the U.S. government brought suit under terms of the Sherman Antitrust Act.

The legal issue was this: The consolidation of the five companies, each of which had made binders, mowers, and rakes, constituted restraint of competition and the creation of a monopoly. In 1914, the court ordered the company to dissolve into its separate parts.

Harvester immediately appealed to the U.S. Supreme Court. Although the importance of the case placed it at the head of the Supreme Court's docket, the case seemed to defy resolution and dragged on for several more years.

Meanwhile in 1918, the United States entered World War I. Besides the Harvester case,

The International 15-30, built between 1918 and 1921, was a modern and capable tractor in its day. It had a governor, an enclosed chain final drive, and after 1920, an air cleaner. It had a four-cylinder en-gine of 693ci that used a high-tension K-W magne-to. The 1918 price, FOB Milwaukee, was just under $2,000.

there were seven other major company antitrust cases awaiting adjudication by the Supreme Court. The government wisely feared that if dissolution was ordered by the Court in any of these cases, the others would automatically follow suit. The result would be total disruption of the nation's war production capability. Therefore, to avoid that eventuality, but to keep its cases viable, the government lawyers petitioned the Court, and were granted an indefinite postponement.

This was more than the long-suffering businessmen at International Harvester could stand. At some future date, complete dissolution of the company could be ordered on the basis of what had occurred in 1902, and this on the basis of testimony possibly twenty years old. Since the company could not contin-ue under this cloud, a settlement was sought.

Thus, in 1918, a consent decree was arranged and later approved by the Court, which in effect sustained the government's view that a monopoly was in place. Harvester agreed to divest itself of the Osborne, Champi-on, and Milwaukee lines of harvesting machines and the plants in which they were made. The dual McCormick and Deering deal-erships were to be eliminated and only one dealership per town was allowed.

Harvester's problems were far from over, however. With the end of the war in Europe and the Bolshevik Revolution in Russia, hor-rendous losses in plants, machinery, and busi-ness had to be written off. No sooner than this was done, the war boom in the agricultural market turned into a depression.

| Rating | Model | Years Built |
|--------|-------|-------------|
| ★★★ | 15-30 | 1921-1928 |
| ★★★ | 10-20 | 1923-1939 |
| ★★★★ | 30 Ind. | 1931-1940 |
| ★★★★ | 20 Ind. | 1923-1940 |
| ★★★★ | 22-36 | 1929-1934 |

# McCormick-Deering: The 15-30, 10-20, and 22-36

*The McCormick-Deering 10-20, 15-30 and the Fordson were, "designed as much for low-cost production as for proper function."*
E.J. Baker, Jr. in *Agricultural Engineering,* June 1931

## The Great Tractor War of the Twenties

"What? What's that? How much? Two hundred and thirty dollars? Well, I'll be. . . What'll we do about it? Do? Why damn it all, meet him, of course! We're going to stay in the tractor business. Yes, cut two hundred and thirty dollars. Both models. Yes, both. And, say, listen, make it good! We'll throw in a plow as well."

That is half of a January 28, 1922 telephone conversation between International Harvester's Chicago and Springfield, Ohio, offices. The words are those of Alexander Legge, the company's gritty general manager, as recorded by Cyrus McCormick III in his book *The Century of the Reaper.* The occasion was a salvo fired by Henry Ford in the Great Tractor War of the twenties. He had just announced a price cut to $395 for a Fordson tractor.

Formed in 1902, International Harvester Company had been under constant legal attack from then until after World War I. The merging of the several companies to form International Harvester was considered by the U.S. Supreme Court to be a patent attempt to eliminate competition. Several states had, at least for a short time, forbidden Harvester to

do business within their borders. All this culminated in 1918 with the consent decree and the sale of three of the several companies making up International Harvester. Also ordered by the Court was the elimination of dual McCormick and Deering dealerships. Now, having survived all that the company found itself under a surprisingly strong competitive attack from the automobile magnate, Henry Ford.

The Ford Motor Company had been organized in 1903, just a year after International Harvester. Henry Ford held only about 26 percent of the stock. By mid-1906, production was up to one hundred cars per day. Ford, who grew up on a farm in Michigan, began experimenting with tractors to "lift the burden of farming from flesh and bones, and place it on steel and motors," as he would later say.

Tractor experiments seemed to diminish somewhat for the next several years as the Model T was developed into the "Universal Car." Production rose steadily from year to year, but it was 1914 that became pivotal in Ford's history. Three significant events occurred in 1914. The first was the $5.00 daily pay rate established on January 12 for Ford production workers. This was an increase from the previous rate of $2.30 per day.

The second event was one that startled the business community just as much as the $5.00 day. It was the institution of the Model T moving assembly line on January 14.

Third, the turmoil in Europe boiled over after the assassination of Austrian Archduke

# Gear Drive Tractor

McCormick-Deering introduced the 15-30 in 1921 in response to inroads into their market share by the Fordson. The 15-30 featured all-gear drive (as opposed to chain drive) and unit construction, which meant that the engine-transmission housings also served as the frame.

Francis Ferdinand, and in August, Germany declared war on Russia and France, beginning World War I.

The effect of these three events caused car production at Ford to skyrocket. The war increased demand for U.S. farm products, and the tractor industry began to expand dramatically as well. With the car business again secure, Henry Ford turned his attention once more to tractors. Ford had the financial resources and the technical talent. His problem was that his fellow directors at the Ford Motor Company did not share his enthusiasm for the tractor business.

In the summer of 1916, prototypes of a new Ford tractor were shown to the public and caused quite a stir among farmers. No longer was this a Model T derivative but an entirely new concept. The engine block, transmission housing, and rear axle housing were the frame of the machine. The father of the design was Eugene Farkas. He had the benefit of the convenient test fields of Ford's newly acquired Fair Lane estate and was able to try out just about every make of tractor. Work on the design had started in 1915 using a Hercules-made engine. This tractor evolved into one closely resembling the production Fordson.

Prior to the U.S. press showing, two tractors were sent to England for testing by the British government. These were the first to bear the name badge "Henry Ford and Son." Tractor work was now being done in a separate factory using Ford's, not Ford Motor Company's, funds. Henry Ford was now fifty-three years old, and his son, Edsel, was twenty-three. A new private company, Henry Ford and Son, Inc., was incorporated July 27, 1917, for the express purpose of mass producing the new low-cost tractor.

# The Powerful New McCormick-Deering 15-30

## A Few 15-30 Features

McCormick-Deering high-tension magneto ignition.

New manifold design, increasing fuel efficiency.

Protected air supply.

Circulating splash engine lubrication.

Filtered fuel supply.

Efficient kerosene carburetion.

Friction-free ball-bearing crankshaft.

Three forward speeds.

Accessible construction.

Removable cylinders.

Replaceable parts throughout

THE POWER in the new 15-30 McCormick-Deering is the symbol of profit farming on a comfortable, efficient scale. With this powerful perfected tractor special opportunities lie ahead of you. Its owner is equipped to rise above the old cramped style of farming—to take *full* advantage of man-power, acreage, crop, and season—to cut to the bone the production costs that eat profit away—*and to build for future expansion.*

This is a *McCormick-Deering* tractor. So you may be positive that its liberal power is matched by new improvements and refinements all along the line. The 4-cylinder power plant, clutch, transmission and differential assemblies, built into a rigid 1-piece main frame, give great reserve strength. All important wearing parts run in a bath of oil. Ball and roller bearings at 34 points add to easy running and long life.

Considering ample power, flexibility, long life, economy, price, service, and easy operation with the equipment which is as important as the tractor itself—here is the tractor of tractors. Ask the dealer about the new 15-30 McCormick-Deering. Other McCormick-Deering Tractors—the 10-20 and the all-purpose Farmall. Catalogs on request.

### INTERNATIONAL HARVESTER COMPANY

606 So. Michigan Ave.  of America  Chicago, Ill.
(Incorporated)

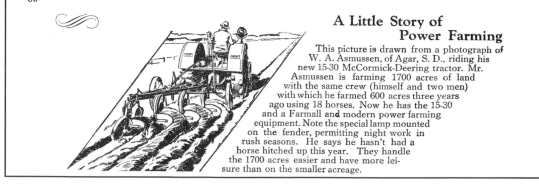

## A Little Story of Power Farming

This picture is drawn from a photograph of W. A. Asmussen, of Agar, S. D., riding his new 15-30 McCormick-Deering tractor. Mr. Asmussen is farming 1700 acres of land with the same crew (himself and two men) with which he farmed 600 acres three years ago using 18 horses. Now he has the 15-30 and a Farmall and modern power farming equipment. Note the special lamp mounted on the fender, permitting night work in rush seasons. He says he hasn't had a horse hitched up this year. They handle the 1700 acres easier and have more leisure than on the smaller acreage.

"Rise above the old cramped style of farming," is the message in this ad. The vignette at the bottom, about Mr. W.A. Asmussen farming 1,700 acres with two men, himself, a light-equipped 15-30, and a Farmall should be a revelation to today's young well-equipped farmers.

Britain, and indeed much of Western Europe, had come to rely on grain imported from the United States, Canada, Australia, and Russia. The low cost of these foods prompted farmers in Europe, and especially in Britain, to turn to raising livestock. When the Turkish Navy blockaded the Dardanelles in 1914, they effectively shut off the flow of wheat from Russia. Later, the German U-boat threat began to curtail grain shipments from the other sources. The British government reacted by establishing tilling goals for arable acreage. Records indicate there were just five hundred tractors in Great Britain in 1914. To achieve their tillage goals, the British Board of Agriculture pushed British tractor makers to the limit of their production capacity. They also ordered the import-

This very early 15-30 is equipped with a rather nice canopy. The 15-30 used a four-cylinder engine with ball-bearing mains on the crankshaft. The 15-30s were built at the Milwaukee works.

A 15-30 seen at the 1993 Eagle River, Wisconsin, show. Although not obvious from this photo, the steering wheel and seat were offset to the right on the 15-30. The four-cylinder vertical valve-in-head engine of the 15-30 had a bore and stroke of 4.5x6in for a piston displacement of 382ci.

# McCormick-Deering 15-30

## A Three-Plow Tractor With
# Ball and Roller Bearings
## *at 29 Points*

In developing the McCormick-Deering 15-30, the Harvester Company has produced a tractor which gives maximum service and economy in operation. The features in design of this tractor are the result of field experience gained through 18 years of contact with tractor farming conditions. Ball and roller bearings have been used at the points of high speed or extreme strain, and all other parts have received the same consideration. The resultant smooth-running, modern tractor meets the many power requirements of the present-day farm.

Practical design, ease of operation and handling, make the McCormick-Deering tractor an ideal three-plow power unit. It also develops a surplus of power to handle a great variety of belt jobs (threshing, silo filling, husking and shredding, feed grinding, etc.) and its smooth, flexible operation and increased speed make it a leader for all kinds of drawbar work.

*You will want to know more about this latest McCormick-Deering tractor. Ask the McCormick-Deering dealer for complete details or write for our new catalog.*

## INTERNATIONAL HARVESTER COMPANY
### Chicago    of America [Incorporated]    USA
*93 Branch Houses and 15,000 Dealers in the United States*

The advantages of ball bearings are touted in this 1923 ad for the 15-30. Notice International Harvester was claiming eighteen years of tractor experience by 1923.

A McCormick-Deering 15-30 pulls a self-powered
combine through a Kansas wheat field, circa 1929.
*Smithsonian Institution*

A lofty perch, right up there with the windmill. This
McCormick-Deering 10-20 serves to attract attention at the Waukee, Iowa, show grounds.

ing of all the Waterloo Boys and International Harvesters they could get, but still food production fell short.

Lord Percival Perry was the chief of Ford's British subsidiary and also a member of the Board of Agriculture. It was Lord Perry who arranged for testing of the Ford's prototype tractors in May of 1916. A panel of five judges, all experienced agriculturists, were favorably impressed by the tractor's durability, ease in starting and handling, and its small size and light weight. They recommended that the British Ford subsidiary go into immediate production. Since Ford had already been granted a license to set up a factory in Cork, Ireland, to produce the Model T, it was decided to use the same site to build the tractor.

Henry Ford was finally in the tractor business. His intention was to begin production in Detroit, as well as in Cork. He was pleased and proud to include Edsel in the business.

German bombing of London and other British cities in June 1917 forced revision of Ford's Cork, Ireland, production plans. All resources were needed to make war machines, such as fighter planes, for the defense of the country. Tractors would have to be imported. On June 28, 1917, Henry Ford announced that he had accepted an order for 6,000 tractors from the British Ministry of Munitions (MOM), to be built in the United States.

Before the end of 1917, 254 MOM tractors were completed. These as yet had no Fordson identification and were hence given the MOM

A nicely restored McCormick-Deering 10-20 on display at the 1994 Waukee, Iowa, show. The 10-20 looked like the 15-30, but was 14in shorter and a ton lighter. Its 284ci four-cylinder engine was slightly larger than that of the Fordson 10-20, which was 251ci. The Fordson weighed 2,970lb in 1923, while the McCormick-Deering 10-20 weighed in at 4,000lb.

This McCormick-Deering 10-20 is driving a shingle mill at the 1994 Waukee, Iowa, show. Raising the side hood helped with the cooling. Note the 6x6 "parking brake."

nickname for the Ministry of Munitions contract. The name "Fordson" actually came from the transatlantic cable address and was a contraction of "Henry Ford and Son." Transatlantic communication was laborious and slow in those days and done in Morse code. Hence, names were shortened and acronyms were used wherever possible. The tractors were not formally called Fordsons until the MOM order was completed and production for the general public began.

By 1920, Fordson production was such that a month's output would exceed the total number of tractors of any of the others for the whole year.

Ford soon found himself, because of the postwar depression, with more tractors than

could be sold. He then started cutting prices to move inventory. The early 'twenties market continued to shrink, further exacerbating what was by this point an industrywide overproduction problem. The other tractor manufacturers, eager to maintain market share, also cut prices, and soon found themselves embroiled in a good old-fashioned price war.

The tractor price war had three prominent effects. First, many farmers took advantage of the below-cost prices to get into power farming. Second, substantial companies were eliminated from the tractor market when they could not get their prices down sufficiently to compete, mainly the "short-line" companies specializing in larger, heavier tractors. Finally, the survivors were forced to copy Ford's pro-

This pristine 10-20 has found its way to England. It is on display at the 1993 Great Dorset Steam Fair.

An International 10-20 gives a plowing demonstration at the 1993 Great Dorset Steam Fair. The 4.25x5in bore and stroke engine of the 10-20 was of the vertical type with valves in-head and had the same type of ball-bearing crankshaft mains as the 15-30.

duction line methods and to redesign their products to be more appealing to the myriad of smaller farmers.

In 1921, the postwar depression caused the downturn in Fordson sales from 71,000 to less than 37,000. Prices were cut throughout the year from $795 to $625, and finally the dramatic cut to $395. Now Fordsons sold. The year 1922 saw production back to around the 70,000 level, and in 1923, more than 100,000 were sold.

International Harvester was on the ropes. They had the obsolete Titan 10-20, the Mogul 8-16, and the International 8-16 in production. Their prices were reduced to $700 for the 10-20s and $670 for the 8-16, still almost double that of the Fordson 10-20. With over 300,000 Fordsons in the field by then they certainly had a measure of experience in their favor. Besides, British records of the government-sponsored wartime plowing indicated that the Fordson plowed more acres per hour at a lower cost for fuel and repairs per acre than the Titan.

Two new McCormick-Deering tractor models were introduced in 1921 and 1922. The Titan and Mogul names were dropped in favor of the McCormick-Deering name, and the models were identified simply as the 15-30 and the 10-20. The prices of these tractors were at the same level as the Titan and Mogul, but they each had a modern, contemporary design.

To counter the onslaught of the Fordson, Harvester issued a challenge throughout the land. Everywhere a Fordson sale was even rumored, the McCormick-Deering dealer dared the Ford dealer to a contest. Grimly they battled for every sale, just like the harvester war of the previous century.

The McCormick-Deering dealers won some of the sales, and lost others, but little by little Harvester won the farmers back from a price-only comparison. Nevertheless, the Fordson greatly outsold all competitors until 1927, when Henry Ford abruptly halted U.S. production. He needed the space, he said, for the new Model A car. Production was transferred to Cork, Ireland, and later to Dagenham, England, where the basic design was continued through 1945.

### The McCormick-Deering Model 15-30

A completely new tractor emerged from the Milwaukee works in late 1921. The factory, too, was completely retooled to take advantage of all the new production line methods pioneered by Ford and the automobile industry. The new McCormick-Deering 15-30 (sometimes called the International 15-30 in the early days) used the unit frame design similar to the Fordson, wherein a single cast iron pan ran from the front axle to the rear

An International Model 20 with unique wheels is on display at the 1993 Great Dorset Steam Fair.

*First-class power delivered to a long list of belt jobs*

# Invest in a McCormick-Deering Tractor
## *for Plowing and Belt Work*

The remarkable new warranty covering the crankshaft and the crankshaft ball bearings in McCormick-Deering Tractors may well prove the deciding factor in *your own investment.* The ironclad agreement, printed below, provides you with a lasting security covering these important parts of the tractor. It is evidence of quality in the entire tractor. It is an indicator of practical design, accurate assembly, generous size of parts, and long life.

Do your plowing speedily and well with a McCormick-Deering and fit your tractor to fall and winter work. McCormick-Deering Tractors are designed to handle belt jobs as you want them handled.

And McCormick-Deering machines are made to work right with tractors. The combination can't be beat.

Stop at the McCormick-Deering dealer's and go over the construction and the features of these tractors. Study the value of replaceable wearing parts, the unit main frame, ball and roller bearings at 28 points, etc. And remember this important fact:

When you buy a McCormick-Deering Tractor you get all necessary equipment—throttle governor, belt pulley, platform, fenders, brake, etc. No extras to pay for.

*Make your power investment safe by placing an order for a McCormick-Deering 15-30 or 10-20 Tractor.*

---

**SPECIAL WARRANTY**
*given every purchaser*

*The seller agrees* to replace free the Two-Bearing Crankshaft in any 10-20 or 15-30 McCormick-Deering tractor, should it break during the life of the tractor, provided the broken parts are promptly returned to the factory or one of the branch houses.

*Further,* the seller agrees to replace free any Crankshaft Ball Bearing in the 10-20 or 15-30 McCormick-Deering tractor, which may break, wear out, or burn out during the life of the tractor, provided that the defective ball bearing is promptly returned to the factory or one of the branch houses.

---

## INTERNATIONAL HARVESTER COMPANY

---

"Make your power investment safe . . ." This 1923 ad emphasizes the special warrantee given on the crankshafts and ball-type main bearings used in the 10-20 and 15-30 tractors. These would be replaced free for the life of the tractor. This could possibly be of interest to current-day owners of these machines, some of which are now more than seventy-three years old.

A McCormick-Deering 10-20 on rubber. Rubber tires became an option in 1923. The big feature that the 10-20 had over the Fordson was the standard rear PTO.

axle. This pan served not only as the frame but also covered the inner workings of the engine, transmission, and differential.

The 15-30 was all new, from the radiator to the wheels. The most interesting feature, however, was the use of ball-bearing mains on the crankshaft. In addition, ball-and-roller bearings were used throughout, a major departure from conventional practices of the day.

The steering wheel and seat were offset to the right for improved visibility. A foot-operated clutch was provided, as was a three-speed transmission. A belt pulley was standard equipment, and the new rear power take-off (PTO) pioneered by Harvester was optional.

The four-cylinder vertical valve-in-head engine of the 15-30 had a bore and stroke of 4.5x6in for a piston displacement of 382ci. Rated engine speed was 1000rpm. The engine was equipped with an Ensign carburetor, a water-washer air cleaner, and a governor built by Harvester. High tension ignition was provided, as was a Harvester-built E4A impulse magneto. Kerosene was the fuel used, after the engine was started on gasoline. The 15-30 weighed just under 6,000lb, double that of the Fordson, but yet far under that of the old Titan.

The McCormick-Deering 22-36 used the same engine as the 15-30, but the bore was increased from 4.5 to 4.75in. The stroke remained 6in. Engine speed was increased to 1050rpm from the previous 1000rpm. Production of the 22-36 began in 1929.

The Model 30 Industrial was generally the same as the 15-30 but with special hard rubber tires. This model should not be confused with the 15-30 Industrial with 10x50in hard rubber tires. Only 530 of the 15-30 Industrial were built between 1930 and 1932, and so rate an extra star. Besides the larger rear wheels, the 15-30 Industrial also used the same round-top fenders as the farm version.

There were also several Orchard variations of the 15-30. One version had a full grille and hood and swept fenders. This one rates an extra star.

### The McCormick-Deering 10-20

This tractor hit the fields in 1923 and was a direct competitor to the Fordson. It looked like the 15-30 but was 14in shorter and a ton lighter. The 284ci four-cylinder engine was slightly larger than the Fordson's 251ci. Both engines were rated at 1000rpm. The Fordson weighed 2,970lb in 1923, while the McCormick-Deering 10-20 weighed in at 4,000lb.

The 4.25x5in bore and stroke engine of the 10-20 was of the vertical type with valves in-head and had the same type of ball-bearing crankshaft mains as the 15-30. The tractor was equipped with a three-speed transmission, a belt pulley, and a water-washer air cleaner, as was the Fordson.

The big feature that the 10-20 had over the Fordson was the standard rear PTO. It was said Harvester didn't know if the PTO binder sold the 10-20, or if it was the other way around. Nevertheless, both sold very well.

An interesting variation of the basic 10-20 was the 10-20 narrow-tread. Introduced in 1925, it had an overall width of just 48in, rather than the standard 60in. The design catered to growers with crop widths too close for the standard model. Give this version an extra star.

Another variation of the basic 10-20 was the Orchard model. This tractor was equipped with fully enclosed rear fenders, a radiator guard, low intake and exhaust pipes, and a lowered steering wheel and seat. Give this type an extra star as well.

Pneumatic rubber tires became an option in 1935 for all of the models.

A Model 20 Industrial was also added to the line in 1923. This was sometimes called the 10-20 Industrial, but it was essentially the same as the farm tractor.

In the sixteen years that the 10-20 was produced, over 215,000 were built, making it the most popular McCormick-Deering tractor up until that time. However, In just three years, 1923, 1924, and 1925, more than 289,000 Fordsons were sold.

### The McCormick-Deering 22-36

The 15-30 was upgraded for the 1929 model year. It was variously called the 22-36, "New" 15-30, and the plain 15-30 by International Harvester throughout its production

The McCormick-Deering 22-36 was virtually the same as the 15-30, except for increases in engine displacement and speed, which gave the tractor the higher rating. The 22-36 demonstrated a rated belt horsepower of 36.15 during testing at the University of Nebraska.

"Big Red" is a McCormick-Deering 22-36 that was seen at the 1994 Freeport, Illinois, show.

run. Production began with Serial Number TG99926, and ended in 1934.

The 22-36 used the same engine as the 15-30, but the bore was increased from 4.5 to 4.75in. The stroke remained 6in. Engine speed was increased to 1050rpm from the previous 1000rpm. A Pomona air cleaner and an oil filter were added.

At maximum pull, over 30 drawbar horsepower was developed, making the 22-36 a full four-bottom tractor. Maximum belt power was listed at 40hp. Harvester prescribed conservative ratings, which enabled the tractor to deliver extremely long life.

After the Fordson was banished to Ireland, International Harvester sold record numbers of their 15-30 model, with sales reaching 35,500 in 1928. The author's granddaughter, Jessica Hope Pripps, age eight, poses by a 15-30 for size comparison.

The Fordson. This is a 1920 version, one of some 75,000 built that year.

# Chapter 3

# The First Farmalls and Their Derivatives

| Rating | Model | Years Built |
|---|---|---|
| ★★★★ | Regular | 1924-1931 |
| ★★★★★ | Reg. Fairway | 1926-1931 |
| ★★ | F-20 | 1932-1939 |
| ★★ | H | 1939-1953 |
| ★★★ | W-4 | 1940-1953 |
| ★★★ | Super H | 1953-1954 |
| ★★★★★ | Super W-4 | 1953-1954 |
| ★★ | 300 | 1954-1956 |
| ★★★ | 300 Utility | 1955-1956 |
| ★★ | 350 | 1956-1958 |
| ★★ | 350 Utility | 1956-1958 |

*The Farmall [was] the first successful attempt at building a genuine all-purpose tractor of the tricycle design.*
R.B. Gray,
*The Agricultural Tractor, 1855-1950*

## Before The Farmall

Between 1915 and 1918, Harvester's experimental engineers worked on the problem of powered cultivation of crops such as corn and cotton. Edward Johnston, head of the Ex-

GP-1430

International Harvester Motor Cultivator, circa 1920. This version has the engine mounted directly to the frame, rather than atop the steering yoke, as in previous versions. Also in this version, the larger front wheels are actually the drivers, and a differential is used.

The 1920 version of the International Harvester Motor Cultivator, the forerunner of the Farmall. Note the steering wheel and driver's seat and also that the final drive is by roller chain.

perimental Department, and a colleague named C.W. Mott filed for a patent for a specialized machine that "pushed" a two-row cultivator. The device, called a Motor Cultivator, had an unusual configuration. A four-cylinder engine rode directly above a pair of close-to-gether rear drive wheels, connected by a vertical driveshaft. This rear element swiveled on the frame around the driveshaft for steering and propulsion, much like an outboard boat motor. The operator sat ahead of the engine with a steering wheel and levers for selecting forward and reverse. The cultivator shovels were mounted ahead of the operator between a pair of nonsteerable, wide-spread front wheels. About 300 of these were sold in 1917 and 1918, but the idea did not catch on. Production ended in 1918. The Motor Cultivator did not sell well because farmers could not afford a machine specifically for cultivating only. But at least the need for an all-purpose machine was being recognized.

## Parallel Efforts

Other companies were also experimenting with power cultivators at the same time, but were no more successful than International Harvester. Then Moline Plow Company introduced its Universal Model D in 1917. It was an unusual contraption, even by the standards of those days. It was, however, the world's first "all-purpose" tractor.

The Universal's dominant feature was a pair of large drive wheels in the front. Dolly-wheels in the back were only used when no implement was installed. Each implement had its own provisions for carrying the back end. The operator sat at the extreme rear, where he had a fairly good view of the implement, which was ahead of him.

Other unique features of the Universal included articulation steering; adjustable drive wheel height, to keep it level when one wheel was in a furrow; a power-lift; electric lights and starter; and an enclosed drivetrain and radiator. The Universal was a success, but its parent company could not survive the hard economic times. The concept of the all-purpose tractor almost died with the Moline Plow Company, as people tended to lump the concept together with the failure of the company.

A machine very similar in concept to the Moline Universal was the Allis-Chalmers 6-12. It was brought out in 1918. The 6-12 was less complicated, however, and things like the starter and lights were left off.

Similar concepts were provided by Parrett, Boring, Allen, Rumely, and others. None of these "all-purpose" tractors were successful in the marketplace because of their poor timing. The inexpensive Fordson simply did not allow room for these more complex ideas. Nevertheless, experiments continued, both at Harvester and the other companies, but only Harvester had the resources and management to see the concept through.

### Development of the Farmall

By 1920, the Motor Cultivator began to change toward the "All-Purpose" tractor configuration. First, the engine was rigidly

A 1921 version of the Motor Cultivator, now called the Farmall by Harvester's Experimental Department. The engine was now parallel to the frame. The driver's position was reversible, so the tractor could be operated in either direction. The chain final drive was replaced by enclosed bull gears. Note the automatic brake cables, a hallmark of later Farmalls.

A studio photo of the 1924 Farmall. Note the special cultivating fenders ahead of the rear wheels.

mounted to the frame, although it was still mounted crosswise. The large front wheels became the drive wheels. The smaller rear wheels became tiller wheels. A cable-winch power lift was provided. Specialized implements were developed in addition to the cultivator.

By October 1920, the steering wheel was made horizontal, and the seat was reversible, so that the machine could be driven in either direction with the operator facing the direction of travel. When the Motor Cultivator was used with mounted implements, the large wheels went first, but when it was used to pull implements or a wagon, the small wheels went first.

In November 1920, the Leroi engine was changed to a Waukesha, and at the same time the engine was changed to a longitudinal mounting. The name Farmall was being used by the experimenters, and the machine began to look like the eventual Farmall.

Implement testing progressed in 1921. The chain drive was replaced by bull gears. The power lift was improved and the tractor was lightened.

It was in 1922 that the tractor price war began. Harvester General Manager Alexander Legge responded to the Fordson's price drop to $395 in three ways. First, he cut the prices of their existing two tractors by the same amount as the Fordson's cut. Next, he launched competitive contemporary tractors, the 15-30 and the 10-30. Finally, Legge commissioned Edward Johnston to go full speed ahead with the Farmall, since Johnston assured him that it could "outdo" the Fordson in every way (except for price, which was initially set at $825).

Legge immediately ordered the construction of twenty more hand-built examples. He also ordered a full complement of implements to be built just for the Farmall. Both were to be ready for thorough testing in 1922. Feedback

The Moline Universal, Model D. A remarkable machine for its time—1917 to 1923. It was indeed the world's first all-purpose tractor. It was also probably the first tractor to have a battery electrical system with starter and lights. The Moline Plow Company purchased the rights to the design from Universal Tractor Company of Columbus, Ohio, in 1914. Allis-Chalmers came out with a similar concept in 1918 each had its impact on the developing Farmall.

*Right*
By January 1927, the Fordson was on the ropes and in this ad International Harvester intends to keep it there. Notice the line about "other men" who lost out by using cheaper, lighter tractors.

### McCormick-Deering Tractors

Two sizes, 10-20 h. p. for 2 plows, and 15-30 h. p. for 3 plows. Fully equipped, 4-cylinder tractors, with ample power at belt, drawbar, and power take-off.

# Next Spring—
## Summer, Autumn, Winter—Profit with
# McCORMICK-DEERING
## Tractor Power

EVERY YEAR McCormick-Deering Tractors stand stronger with the farmers. The name McCormick-Deering has become the symbol of reliable power farming because it stands for carefully built, practical, many-sided, long-lived farm power.

That is so in your community and everywhere. Men who have used International Harvester tractors — for months or for years — are steadfast friends of McCormick-Deering farm power. They will recommend McCormick-Deering when you come to buy. Other men, who risked using cheaper, lighter tractors, found themselves underpowered. They fell short of reaching full production with the least possible labor and in the shortest possible time. After this experience they were ready for new and better power. There are thousands like these, too, who will recommend McCormick-Deering when you make your power investment.

McCormick-Deering gives you your choice of three tractors— the McCormick-Deering 10-20, the 15-30, and the new all-purpose row-crop tractor, the FARMALL. All are quality tractors, built to last many years. Any one of them will work for you with *drawbar, belt,* and *power take-off* the year around. Any one of them will cut your producing costs and add to your profits. Look them over at the dealer's store. *Catalog will be sent on request.*

INTERNATIONAL HARVESTER COMPANY
606 S. Michigan Ave.  OF AMERICA  Chicago, Ill.
(Incorporated)

### The FARMALL!

The remarkable new 4-cylinder McCormick-Deering FARMALL, designed to handle cultivating and planting of row crops, as well as all other farm power work.

# Most Popular — Most Profitable — Best
# McCORMICK-DEERING *for 1927!*

A Farmall Regular provides belt power at a Midwest thresheree. After the second Farmall, the F-30, was introduced in 1931, the original Farmall became known as the Regular. Prior to this time, the original was simply known as the Farmall.

to the design team resulted in a few more changes to the tractor and implements and in many new implements. Cost figures acquired by the field men indicated a six-to-one reduction in planting, tilling, and harvesting costs versus horse farming.

The Farmall sales exceeded expectations in 1925. By 1926 the new Rock Island, Illinois, plant was in operation and Farmalls were rolling out the door. Even at its peak production, before the crash of '29, only about 24,000 Farmalls per year were built. This was a far

This nice Farmall F-20 with round-spoke wheels and rubber tires appeared at the 1994 Waukee, Iowa, show.

cry from the 100,000 Fordsons built per year during Ford's peak years. Late in 1927, Henry Ford abruptly transferred Fordson production to Cork, Ireland, and its impact on the U.S. market dwindled to almost nothing. Ford said he needed the space for car production. The truth was, however, that the Fordson needed a complete redesign to be competitive with the Farmall.

By the end of the 1920s, International Harvester Company was clearly again at the top of the farm implement industry. It enjoyed sales three times that of its nearest competitor, Deere & Company of Moline, Illinois.

The introduction of the Farmall was an enormous triumph for Harvester, and not only because of its victory over the Fordson. It also overcame sticky resistance to the concept

The Farmall F-20, introduced in 1932, was a considerable update from the Farmall Regular. It had increased displacement and power, it was longer, and it had a four-speed transmission.

of the all-purpose tractor both within IHC and in the industry at-large. When the first Farmall rolled out, there was no advertising blitz, no ceremony, not even a press conference. Harvester management was so cautious that initially sales were to be made only in Texas—to prevent corporate embarrassment if they were not successful.

When the Farmall appeared, it seemed top-heavy and fragile as compared to standard-tread tractors of the day. The Farmall and its imitators sold so well that they changed the concept of the conventional tractor to that of the row-crop, or high tricycle configuration. This remained so into the 1960s when chemical herbicides replaced the need

By 1939, the last year that it was built, F-20 Farmalls were mature, respected machines. Almost 150,000 were built, shattering all previous McCormick-Deering model production records.

for crop cultivators, and wide-fronts again became popular.

### The Farmall Regular

Note, first of all, the Regular was not called the Regular until the Farmall F-30 came out in 1931. When there was only one model, it was simply called the Farmall.

It wasn't, in fact, officially called the Farmall until 1923 when that name was given by a corporate naming committee and registered as a trademark. Twenty-two copies of the 1923 version were made and sent to various places for testing. It is interesting that they were sent to places where the McCormick-Deering 10-20 was not selling well, as management did not want farmers delaying purchases to wait for the Farmall.

Implements were sent along with the tractors. Field engineers went, too. Plows, harrows

Don Wolf, a retired Fort Wayne, Indiana, businessman and now farmer, poses with his 1939 Farmall F-20. Besides the nicely restored Farmall, Wolf's collection includes a big Rumely, several green tractors, numerous cars and a completely restored 1914 Stegman truck.

# FARMALL Plowing and Belt Work Simply Can't Be Surpassed!

THERE is enthusiasm for the work of the FARMALL wherever this perfected tractor appears. On all crops, on all jobs in field and barnyard, it shows the power farmer *something new in handling and efficiency*.

*Plowing* is one of its strongest suits. The FARMALL owner goes out to tackle that once-dreaded job with interest and good humor. He has learned that FARMALL and its plow will move handily and rapidly over the fields and leave well-turned furrows behind, in ideal shape for the operations and the crops to follow.

On belt work it is the same. We have dozens of positive letters from owners.

D. M. Hastings of Atlanta, Ga., writes, "You deserve a pat on the back for the FARMALL. Please do not thank me for this as it is well deserved." He has used his FARMALL on every kind of work including many belt jobs.

Remember that the Harvester engineers devoted several years to working out this *all-purpose, all-crop, all-year design*. They tried out thoroughly *every* type of design. When FARMALL was *right for all drawbar, belt and power take-off work* they offered it to the farmer. The FARMALL is *the one all-purpose tractor that plants and cultivates, too.* It is the feature of power farming today.

*Begin by asking the McCormick-Deering dealer where you can see a FARMALL on the job*

## INTERNATIONAL HARVESTER COMPANY
of America
(Incorporated)

606 So. Michigan Ave.          Chicago, Illinois

. . . And next spring your FARMALL will be all ready to go at the PLANTING and CULTIVATING jobs. It's that kind of a tractor!

The F-20 can generally be distinguished from the Regular by a shorter air intake stack. The power of the F-20 made it capable of handling a 14in two-bottom plow. It could plow about seven acres in a ten-hour day.

*Left*
This 1927 ad says the Farmall farmer tackles the dreaded plowing task with "good humor." Makes some of us who never plowed with horses wonder if we missed something.

of various kinds, planters, and cultivators were tried. Later in the year such items as crop dusters and mowers were added. Then came more plows, such as hillers, middle breakers, and PTO harvesters.

The 1923 version included a unique wire and pulley affair that automatically applied one brake when the steering wheel was turned to its limit. This was called "Triple Control,"

49

The F-20 could handle a 22in threshing machine under most conditions. The speed of the belt pulley was reduced from the Regular's 690rpm to 650rpm on the F-20 to produce a belt speed very close to the industry standard of 2,395ft per minute. A 1939 F-20 is shown.

and it allowed the operator to lift the implement, handle the clutch, and change directions at the end of the row.

Against the better judgment of many of Harvester's marketing men, the company decided on a production run of two hundred Farmalls for 1924. The Marketing Department believed the new tractor would just take sales away from the proven 10-20. Nevertheless, the price was set arbitrarily at a low $825, which was about the same as the 10-20 at that time.

The 1924 model had several improvements. The rear axle housing was made heavier, as were the rear wheel hubs, transmission case, and drawbar. The frame was also strengthened and made from box-section steel, rather than channel steel. The 1924 models used a tall air intake stack at the left side of the engine. A flannel cloth covered the intake in the first effort to get cleaner air for the engine.

In 1925, and on, an oil bath air cleaner was employed, mounted in front of the radiator.

The price was raised to $925 for 1925. A total of 837 were built, with only minor changes in configuration from the 1924 model. Harvester marketing people wanted to avoid conflict with the McCormick-Deering 10-20, and so it was decided not to give the Farmall a horsepower rating. After the tractor was tested at the University of Nebraska (Test Number 117), however, horsepower figures were soon well known.

Although the Farmall had a smaller engine (22ci for the Farmall versus 284ci for the 10-20) the power was almost the same at 20hp. The Farmall engine had a rated speed of 1200rpm, rather than 1000rpm as on the 10-20, and thus produced more power for its size. Fuel for both was kerosene. As tested, the Farmall was almost 100lb heavier than the 10-20.

F-20 Farmalls were available with rubber tires from the factory in 1936. Also, all Farmalls were painted gray through most of 1936.

It was about 1,000lb heavier than the Fordson. A three-speed transmission was provided.

The Rock Island, Illinois, plant was ready to begin mass production of the Farmall in 1926. Alexander Legge had purchased the structure (which oddly, had been the factory for the Moline Universal) and had it refurbished for mass production of the new tractor. It went on line in time for 4,418 Farmalls to be completed yet that year. No longer was there any doubt about the acceptance of the all-purpose tractor or any concern about hurting 10-20 sales. Now the problem was producing enough Farmalls to meet the demand.

By 1930, two hundred Farmalls per day were coming off the line. Total produced reached 100,000 that year. The team at International Harvester had beaten off the challenge of the Fordson and had changed farming just as surely as did the Fordson. While

Instrumentation on the F-20 was sparse, to say the least. Hand brakes, (the lever with the knob on the left), were used until 1939, when dual foot brakes, both on the right side, were introduced .

The Farmall H, introduced in 1939, barely changed in outward appearance, even through the Super H period, which ended in 1953.

there were many horses providing farm power up through World War II, the appearance of the Farmall spelled the end of horse farming.

### The Fairway

A Fairway model was offered in addition to the regular Farmall. The Fairway was the same except for its special wide, flat steel 40x16in rear wheels and 25x8in front wheels customized for intended duties on estates and golf courses. This version also found use at airports and factories. The special wheels were used with and without turf spud-lugs.

*Left*
Farmall ads stressed personal testimonies. This one is from 1929.

Unfortunately, production records do not differentiate between the Regular and the Fairway; therefore, it is only the special wheels that set them apart.

### The Farmall F-20

During 1932 the Farmall Regular was updated and given the designation F-20. The engine bore and stroke were now 3.75x5in as in the Regular, but the tractor was slightly stronger with about ten percent more power.

A four-speed transmission replaced the three-speed unit of the Regular. The speed of the belt pulley was reduced from 690rpm to 650rpm to produce a belt speed very close to the industry standard of 2,395ft per minute. Weight grew because of these changes. The F-20 can generally be distinguished from the Regular by its shorter air intake stack.

The power of the F-20 made it capable of

The Farmall H, introduced in 1939, was a replacement for the F-20, and the styling was by industrial designer Raymond Lowey. Shown is a Farmall Super H wide-front.

handling a 14in two-bottom plow. Thus equipped, it could plow about seven acres in a ten-hour day. The F-20 could handle a 22in threshing machine under most conditions as well.

The F-20 was available in regular and narrow versions. Each version had two optional rear wheel treads. The regular version rear wheels could be at either 74in or 83in. The narrow version could be set at either 77in or 57in. By 1935, the narrow version could be ordered with a wide front axle, and thus equipped, would rate an extra star. Also available that year was a rubber tire option. During 1938, a wide version was offered with dished cast wheels that could reach a 96in width. An adjustable wide front axle was available with that version. A single wheel front end was also an option instead

of dual narrow wheels that year. Give these an extra star, as well.

All Farmalls were painted battleship gray until late 1936, when Farmall red was introduced.

Production of the F-20 ended in 1939, although tractors were available from stock during part of 1940. Almost 150,000 were built, shattering all previous McCormick-Deering model production records.

### The Farmall H

The Model H Farmall, introduced in 1939, was the replacement for the F-20. Industrial designer Raymond Lowey had been engaged by Harvester management to not only restyle the tractor line but to suggest a total redesign so that form followed function. The styling took the form of smoothly contoured bright red sheet metal and a purposeful new grille. The new science of ergonomics was applied. A foot clutch was on the left side of the ample platform, and dual brake pedals were on the right. Gone was the old cable steering brake setup, and a five-speed transmission replaced the four-speed unit of the F-20.

A new engine was developed for the H. It was a more modern, higher speed unit of 152ci displacement, operating at a rated speed of 1650rpm. As such, it was in the 25hp class, the same as the older F-20. This power gave the H the capability to handle a 14in two-bottom plow or to drive a 22in thresher with relative ease.

The new H featured key-axle rear wheel width adjusting. The spread could be changed from as close as 44in to as wide as 80in.

The beautifully restored Farmall H seen here is at the 1993 Eagle River, Wisconsin, show.

A 1939 Farmall H, owned by Brett Shoger, shown at the 1994 Sandwich, Illinois, show. Even after fifty-five years, it looks quite modern.

The Model HV is the high-crop version of the Far-mall H. Note the high arched front axle. A roller chain final drive also raises the rear axle. This 1948 Farmall HV is owned by Larry Eipers of Minooka, Illinois.

The H was introduced at the same time as the big brother Model M. They shared the same frame layout so that mounted implements were interchangeable.

Most Model Hs were equipped with gasoline engines, although distillate versions were available. Most were equipped with rubber tires, except for those affected by the rubber shortages of World War II. In the war years, many Model Hs were sold on steel, or with rubber fronts and steel rears. An H on full, original steel is worth an extra star. Most Model Hs were of the tricycle configuration, but wide-front and high-crop (HV) versions were available. A wide-front H rates an extra star; an HV rates two extra stars.

The Model H, and the big-brother M, used water pump cooling systems. The earliest of these did not have pressure radiator caps.

## The McCormick W-4, OS-4, and O-4 Models

The W-4 was a standard-tread version of the Model H. It was introduced in 1940, re-

Mandy Barrows, age 10, handles the 1942 Farmall H and loader for her father, John Barrows. The Barrows family lives in Rochelle, Illinois. Mandy's grandfather, Clyde Barrows is well known for his big Case steam engine, which appears annually at the Franklin Grove, Illinois, show.

The International W-4 Standard is the standard-tread version of the Farmall H. This one is on display at the 1993 Great Dorset Steam Fair in England.

The W-4 standard-tread version of the Model H was first introduced in 1940, replacing the old Model 10-20. It was produced until 1953, and then as the Super W-4 in 1953 and 1954.

placing the last remnants of the old 10-20. It was equipped with the same 152ci four-cylinder engine and five-speed transmission. As with the H, electric starters and lights were a popular option.

The OS-4 (Orchard Special) was essentially the same as the W-4, except the air intake and exhaust pipe were relocated below the tractor to prevent entanglement with the tree limbs. The O-4 model was the same in that regard, but in addition, had extended streamlined fenders over the rear wheels. The option-

al headlights for both Orchard versions were mounted below the grille, to avoid being damaged by the tree limbs.

The OS-4 version of the W-4 rates an extra star. The O-4, with the big fenders, gets two extra stars. All versions on original full steel wheels rate an additional star.

### The Farmall Super H

In 1953, the Model H was upgraded to the Super H. The big difference was an increase in engine displacement to 164ci from the previ-

Standing proudly in the display row at the 1993 Freeport, Illinois, show, this W-4 appears to be freshly restored. The W-4 is equipped with the same 152ci four-cylinder engine and four-speed transmission as the H.

The W-4 Standard was also available as the OS-4 Orchard Special and the O-4 Orchard with the extended streamlined fenders over the rear wheels. In 1953, all these were upgraded to the Super versions with an increase in engine displacement to 164ci from the previous 152.1ci.

ous 152.1ci. The engine was rated at 1650rpm. Horsepower increased to over 30 to give the Super H a true two-bottom 16in or three-bottom 14in capacity. Only a gasoline version was available.

These changes added approximately 700lb to the basic weight of the tractor, bringing it up to 4,400lb. For serious pulling, the Super H could be ballasted to around 8,000lb.

The Super H was available in tricycle, adjustable wide-front (one extra star), or fixed wide-front high-crop (two extra stars) versions. Hydraulics were optional.

The Super H was equipped with the new International Harvester disk brakes. These brake units employed ball-ramp self-energizing devices in which the motion of the tractor tended to increase clamping forces on the disks.

## The McCormick Super W-4

Production of the standard-tread model of the H line continued into the Super era. The Super W-4 got the same engine improvements and the five-speed transmission.

This tractor featured 13-26 rear tires. Its basic weight was just over 4,200lb, but that could be nearly doubled with ballast. As with the Super H, steel wheels were not an option for the Super W-4.

Production of standard-tread tractors began to be greatly diminished by the 1950s, mostly because of the rising popularity of utility tractors. Therefore, there were only

This Farmall 300 is still at work in Wisconsin's Door County peninsula. The 300 was built between 1954 and 1956. To be correct, however, the white grille and side panels are not appropriate for the Model 300 but are correct for the later Model 350.

For sale along the road in Northwestern Wisconsin, this Farmall 300 appears to need little but a fresh paint job. A displacement increase to 169ci from the 164ci of the Super H and a speed increase to 1750rpm brought the 300 up to almost 40hp.

about 4,000 Super W-4s made. This accounts for their collectability and their five-star rating.

## The Farmall 300

Until 1954, improvements in the mid-sized Farmall line had mainly been evolutionary, but the Model 300 represented a steep increase in everything from appearance to utility.

A displacement increase to 169ci and a speed increase to 1750rpm brought the 300's power up to almost 40hp. The tractor was now in the big leagues regarding implements such as mowers and harrows. It was rated as a three-plow tractor. Basic weight was over 5,000lb without ballast. Some 4,000lb of ballast could be added to the rear wheels.

The 300 received the new Fast-Hitch im-

The Farmall 350, produced between 1956 and 1958, was externally different from the 300 only in that the grille and side panels were painted white. Internally, a 1/16in increase in the engine bore gave a 3hp increase, putting it over 40hp.

Harvester collector Larry Johnson shows off his
1957 Farmall 350 at the 1994 Sandwich, Illinois,
show.

plement lift, which made changing from one
implement to another faster and easier. The
300 also had a live PTO and the torque amplifier (TA).

The torque amplifier was a Harvester innovation. The name became more-or-less
generic as other brands picked up the idea. In
operation, the torque amplifier provided a
1.482:1 ratio increase when actuated, providing an on-demand power downshift of about
33 percent. This was usually enough to get
through a tough spot without stopping to
shift the main transmission down. It func-
tioned much like "passing gear" in a car's au-

tomatic transmission. The TA feature employed a clutch-controlled planetary gearset
that provided direct drive and an "underdrive" ratio for each of the transmission
gears, effectively giving the tractor ten speeds
forward and two in reverse.

The 300 was offered with options that rate
an extra one and a half stars to the collector:
the high-clearance style and the LPG engine
version.

### The International 300 Utility

Real competition for all came in June of
1939 when a specter of the Twenties Tractor

This Farmall 350 has obviously spent a lot of time out doors, but otherwise, appears to be in good condition. It was being used regularly to power a pump via its PTO. It was seen near Cherry Valley, Illinois.

War arose: Henry Ford was back in the U.S. tractor business. His new Model 9N tractor, incorporating the Ferguson implement system and weighing only 2,500lb, was selling for a mere $600. It could plow more than twelve acres in a normal day, pulling two "fourteens." This was better acreage than the 1939 F-30 could do at a price of over $1,200. The 9N was not a row-crop tractor in the true sense of the word, but its adjustable wide front did incorporate downward-extending kingpins that gave it fairly good crop clearance.

This front axle arrangement and adjustable rear wheel spacing, along with a fairly low-slung cross-section and integral hydraulics for mounted implements, became known as the utility tractor configuration.

A characteristic of the Farmall Regular is the use of exposed steering gears. On subsequent Farmalls, these were enclosed.

This freshly restored Farmall H was seen at the Stephenson County Antique Engine Club's Freeport, Illinois, show in July 1994.

Just as the Farmall changed the idea of the conventional tractor to that of the row-crop type in the 1920s, so the 9N Ford-Ferguson began to change it to the utility type.

The International 300 Utility was the first utility type tractor for International Harvester. Internally, it was basically the same as the Farmall 300, except the engine was rated at 2000rpm rather than at 1750rpm. It was low, stable, and maneuverable. With Fast-Hitch implements, it could do just about any job on the farm. The utility tractor also found much use as a loader tractor with a front-mounted hydraulic bucket.

The 300 Utility was available with the same LPG engine as the Farmall 300. This version of the 169ci engine had a compression ratio of 8.75:1 in order to take full advantage of the fuel. The LPG International 300 Utility rates two stars over the gasoline version.

**The Farmall 350**

The main external difference between the Farmall 300 and the Farmall 350, produced between 1956 and 1958, was just that the grille and side panel were painted white. Internally, a 1/16in increase in the engine bore gave a 3hp increase, putting it over 40hp. The LPG fuel version was still available, but new for the 350 was a 193ci diesel by Continental. These later two engine versions rate two extra stars.

### The International 350 Utility

The 350 Utility got the same changes as the Model 350 Farmall, including the white grille and side panel, the displacement increase for the gasoline and LPG versions, and the new Continental diesel engine. Also new for the 350 Utility was the power width adjustment system for the rear wheels.

The popularity of the 350 Utility tractor is shown by the fact that the number produced exceeded the number of Farmall 350s during the last year of production. Therefore, both types rate the same number of stars. The LPG and diesel International 350s rate an extra star.

This 1942 Farmall H is being tested on the dynamometer at the 1994 Freeport, Illinois, show. Operation of the tractor seems to be a family affair.

International W-4s were built from 1940 to 1953, but are nevertheless quite rare, especially in row-crop country. This one appears to be in nearly perfect condition.

The OS-4 Orchard Special was essentially the same as the W-4, except the air intake and exhaust pipe were relocated below the tractor to prevent entanglement with the tree limbs. It was also narrower and had a hand clutch. Jon Kayser of Dell Rapids, South Dakota, owns this rare beauty.

This view shows how narrow the OS-4 Orchard Special actually is. This enhanced the tractor's ability to maneuver among the trees.

# Chapter 4

# The Big Farmalls and Their Derivatives

| Rating | Model | Years Built |
|---|---|---|
| ★★★ | F-30 | 1932-1939 |
| ★★★ | W-30 | 1932-1940 |
| ★★ | M | 1939-1952 |
| ★★★ | W-6 | 1940-1953 |
| ★★★ | Super M | 1952-1954 |
| ★★★★ | Super W-6 | 1952-1954 |
| ★★★ | 400 | 1954-1956 |
| ★★★★★ | W-400 | 1955-1956 |
| ★★★ | 450 | 1956-1958 |
| ★★★★★ | W-450 | 1956-1958 |

*No development in the industry was regarded with more distrust, and wholesale opposition than the suggested general purpose tractor . . . The opposition came more from farm implement manufacturers' home organizations than from the field. .*
From an article in the March 1931 issue of
*Agricultural Engineering*

The competition the Fordson stirred up in the early twenties provided the incentive International Harvester needed to develop a machine that could do what the Fordson could not. The Fordson was not useful for cultivating crops such as corn and cotton. It did not have a driveshaft power take-off, and therefore was not

The Farmall F-30 was the first variation of designer Bert Benjamin's original Farmall. It was 33 percent more powerful than the original and could handle a three-bottom plow in most soils.

suitable for the new harvesting implements. Most of all, while it could replace some horses on a farm, it could not replace them all.

As early as 1910, Harvester engineers had talked to General Manager Alexander Legge about a more versatile tractor. The head of the Experimental Department at the time was a young engineer named Edward Johnston, who had started with the McCormick outfit during the Harvester War period. He had been instrumental in keeping McCormick's products competitive with patents covering mowers, knotters, binders, headers, and the like.

Edward Johnston's activities with motor vehicles began with a machine he made for himself before the turn of the century, which he called an "Auto Buggy." For many years he commuted between his home and the plant in his machine. In the early 1900s, Cyrus McCormick became interested in the Buggy and commissioned Johnston to make one after the fashion of a farm wagon, capable of hauling a ton of cargo. This machine hit the market in 1906 and was the forerunner of the International truck.

Johnston and his team, which included such geniuses as Bert R. Benjamin and C.W. Mott, had some ideas for improving the tractor's utility. Their first accomplishment was the invention of the rear driveshaft-type power take-off (PTO). This was incorporated into their 8-16 tractor, and subsequently, was standard equipment on the new 10-20.

The team also worked on and tested many variations on the all-purpose Motor Cultivator theme. Around 1919 the name Motor Cultivator disappeared and the company began to use the name Farmall. As they went along, they kept General Manager Legge and Chairman McCormick informed, but no official corporate interest was shown.

In July 1921, when the Fordson onslaught threatened the whole International Harvester empire, Legge called in Johnston and asked him what had happened to the ten or so all-purpose tractor designs. By then, Johnston and his team had focused on one type, of which several prototypes existed. Johnston insisted that this all-purpose Farmall could beat the Fordson in every way. When told this, Legge

This January 1936 ad stresses planning tractor purchases for the upcoming season to avoid being disappointed, like farmers were the previous year when the supply could not keep up with demand.

The Farmall F-30 on steel cost a little over $1,000 in 1934. This one with rubber tires was priced at $1,225.

Master Case tractor collector John Davis sits on his grandfather's F-30 Farmall. John farms 1,500 acres near Maplewood, Ohio, but also finds time to be a restorer-collector. John, his brother, and son have a nice variety of restored tractors.

immediately ordered the construction of twenty more hand-built examples. He also ordered a full complement of implements to be built customized for the Farmall. Both were to be ready for thorough testing in 1922. Production began in limited fashion in 1924.

The Farmall sales exceeded expectations in 1925. By 1926 the new Rock Island, Illinois, plant was in operation and Farmalls were rolling out the door.

To say that the Farmall was a success would be an understatement. The farmers loved them. Most, however, hedged their bets and kept their horses for another season. Few did after the first year. Sales of the new tractor, while not disappointing to Harvester, were kept artificially low by the inability of the farmer of the time to come up with the cash for the purchase. Lack of real faith in the Far-

This F-30 is now in the hands of a collector and will soon undergo restoration. The F-30 was longer than the Farmall Regular and almost a ton heavier.

mall by IHC management also left the production facilities somewhat strained and prevented lowering of the price through the full impact of true mass production. Nevertheless, the Farmall assembled well, worked well on the farm, sold well, and made a profit for the stockholders.

As stated in Chapter 3, the first Farmall did not have an identifying number or letter. It was simply the Farmall. By 1931, the forces of competition, namely John Deere, were calling for a more powerful version. John Deere had come out with the faltering Model GP in 1928. It was a good tractor designed to counter Harvester's Farmall. Its main problem was in its tools  it was designed for three-row planting and tilling—but farmers wanted either two or four. By 1930, these problems were, for the most part, solved, but the GP was given a displacement increase that gave it more power

The F-30 was a three-plow tractor. It was designed for the larger row crop farms where the big standard-tread machines had already been in use. It used the 4.25x5in bore and stroke engine of the McCormick-Deering 10-20 tractor rated at 1150rpm.

than the Farmall. It was at this point that Harvester management decided to come out with a second, larger, Farmall.

### The Farmall F-30

The first variation of designer Bert Benjamin's successful Farmall was the more powerful Model F-30, brought out in 1932. While the Farmall Regular was considered a two-plow tractor, the new F-30 was a three-plow tractor. It was designed for the larger farms in row-crop country where the big standard-tread machines had already been in use. The idea was not so much to replace horses as to replace competitive tractors.

The new F-30 was 1ft longer than the Regular and 3/4 of a ton heavier, with a basic

The McCormick-Deering W-30 was a standard-tread version of the Farmall F-30. However, when the F-30 was upgraded to a four-speed unit, the W-30 stayed with the three-speed transmission. The W-30 was used as an industrial tractor but without a

special model number. Likewise, there was an Orchard version, but it too was not given a special designation. Slightly more than 32,000 W-30s were built between 1932 and 1940.

weight of 5,500lb. It could plow almost an acre per hour and burned about 1 1/2 gallons of kerosene per hour.

The engine of the F-30 was based upon the very successful engine in the 10-20 conventional tractor. It used the same 4.25x5in bore and stroke and was rated at 1150rpm. Otherwise, the F-30 kept the same configuration as the F-20. The steering and brake arrangement continued; the engine placement and the four-speed transmission also continued, as did splash lubrication and all-gear drive. By 1934, variations included a wide-front axle arrangement, which rates an extra star for the collector, and a special high-crop tractor with a fixed wide-front, which rates two extra stars. In 1936, pneumatic tires and electric lighting became options. Red paint became standard, replacing the previous battleship gray. With factory rubber tires, a high-speed fourth gear could be installed. A power lift was available. After 1938, the power lift was hydraulically operated.

Only about 28,000 F-30s were produced— far fewer than the number of F-20s, and therefore, it rates an extra star.

### The McCormick-Deering W-30

The McCormick-Deering W-30 was a standard tread version of the Farmall F-30. Production of the W-30 overlapped that of the Model 22-36, which was slightly more powerful and which continued in production until 1934. The W-30 was about $175 cheaper than the 22-36's price of $1,150. Powerwise, the W-30 was a close match for the 15-30, which was discontinued in 1928.

The steering wheel and seat were offset slightly to the right for improved visibility. The W-30 kept the three-speed transmission until 1938, when a four-speed unit became standard.

The W-30 industrial tractor was known as the I-30. An orchard version was also built,

*Right*
This wartime ad by Ethyl Corporation suggests converting kerosene tractors to gasoline during dealer overhaul.

Patrick H. Riley is shown driving his 1952 Farmall
M, which he bought new in 1952. The big M is
pulling a PTO baler.

The Farmall M was the top of the Farmall line from
1939 to 1954, replacing the F-30. The M was popular with large-acreage row-crop farmers and sales
averaged over 22,000 units per year.

The Farmall M used a 247.7ci four-cylinder engine. At its rated 1450rpm, the engine produced enough power to easily handle three 16in bottoms. Because fuel consumption was so low the M could also be used economically for lighter chores.

The Farmall M was powered by either a high-compression gasoline engine or a distillate version with lower compression. Rubber tires were standard, except for wartime, when quite a few were delivered on steel.

but no special model number was issued. The orchard version is identified by its sweeping rear fenders and rates two extra stars to the collector.

Slightly more than 32,000 W-30s were built between 1932 and 1940—about 4,000 more than the number of F-30s produced.

## The Farmall M

The mighty M was the top of the Farmall line from 1939 to 1954, replacing the F-30. The M was popular with large-acreage row-crop farmers whose sales averaged over 22,000 units per year. The big 247.7ci engine, loafing along at only 1450rpm, produced enough power to easily handle three 16in bottoms. Because fuel consumption was so low, the M could be used economically for lighter chores.

Options for the M included the Lift-All hydraulic system, a belt pulley, PTO, starter and lights, rubber tires, and a swinging drawbar.

The diesel MD was added to the line in 1941 and rates an extra star. The block part of the MD's engine was essentially the same as the gasoline engine. In the case of the diesel, aluminum pistons were generally used, and piston rings were thicker. A five main bearing crankshaft was used rather than three, as in the gasoline version. The head was, of course, completely different in that the compression ratio was more than doubled to 14.2:1. In addition, the head contained the diesel starting system that allowed the engine to be started on gasoline and, after things were sufficiently warm, to be switched over to diesel.

This Farmall M was seen at the 1994 Waukee, Iowa, show. Notice that it does not have a belt pulley. Options for the M included a belt pulley, the Lift-All hydraulic system, PTO, starter and lights, and a swinging drawbar.

The Super M replaced the M in 1952. Engine displacement was increased to 263.9ci, giving the Super M a 22 percent power boost in the gasoline version and a 32 percent boost in the diesel version.

This Farmall Super M stands in the January snow near Wausau, Wisconsin, waiting for the spring plowing season. It has been restored by Bronowicz Bros. Tractors and Equipment of Marathon, Wisconsin. Besides the gasoline and diesel versions of the Super M, an LPG-fuel option was also available. The Super M was built from 1952 through 1954.

The Super M-TA Farmall was only offered in 1954. The "TA" stands for torque amplifier. The torque amplifier provided a 1.482:1 ratio increase when actuated, providing an on-demand power downshift to get through tough spots without stopping to shift the main transmission down. It made the Super M-TA a ten-speed tractor.

The engine was started on gasoline with the diesel governor control lever (throttle) closed and with the compression relief lever pulled. Pulling the compression release accomplished four things: the combustion chamber was enlarged providing a compression ratio of 6.4:1; intake air was diverted through the starting carburetor; the ignition circuit was completed; and the carburetor float was released, allowing the carburetor to fill with fuel. After a minute of gasoline operation, the com-

pression relief lever would be pushed in and the diesel throttle opened. Operation would thereby be switched to diesel.

Although the diesel MD cost one and a half times as much as the gasoline M, most farmers found it well worth the investment. The MD used about a third less fuel than the frugal M.

The M could be ordered in high-crop, wide-front, or tricycle configurations. The high-crop, MV rates two extra stars. Give one extra star for the wide-front version. In the early days of the M, rubber tires were an option, although steel wheels were rare. An M on full steel rates an extra star.

### The Farmall Super M

In 1952, the Super M replaced the M. Engine displacement was upped to 263.9ci, giving the Super M a 22 percent power boost in the gasoline version and a 32 percent boost in the diesel version. It was also available with an LPG (liquefied petroleum gas) engine, which was a popular low-cost alternative in many areas during the fifties The LPG engine rates an extra star. In addition to low cost, using LPG meant the elimination of sludge and deposits in the engine and the doubling of the engine's life between overhauls.

The Farmall Super MD was among the most popular and successful of the American three-plow tractors. Fuel economy and modern features keep most of them in service forty-plus years after their initial delivery.

Harvester announced its series of standard tractors in 1940. These included the W-6, shown, the W-4 variation of the row crop Model H, and the big 50hp

W-9. The W-6 was the standard tread version of the Farmall M.

A Super MV (high-crop) model was also available and rates two extra stars.

The big news with the Super M was the M-TA version in 1954, with the TA letters standing for torque amplifier. This accessory earns an extra star for the tractor. The torque amplifier was a Harvester innovation in farm tractors and the name became more or less generic as other brands picked up the idea. In operation, the torque amplifier provided a 1.482:1 ratio increase when actuated, providing an on-demand power downshift to get through a tough spot without stopping to shift the main transmission down. The TA feature employed a clutch-controlled planetary gearset that provided direct drive and an underdrive ratio for each of the transmission gears, effectively giving the Super M-TA ten speeds forward and two in reverse.

The M-TA was the first Farmall with a live PTO.

The W-6 used the same engine and five-speed transmission as the Farmall M. The original engine was the 247.7ci four-cylinder overhead valve unit. This was followed by the 263.9ci engine in the Super Series. Displacement of the diesel engines was the same as those for gasoline, distillate, and LPG. Besides compression ratio differences for each type, the diesel was considerably beefed up and had Harvester's patented gasoline starting system.

Some 50,000 W-6, Super W-6, and W-6-TA tractors were built between 1940 and 1954. This one found its way to England and was seen at the 1993 Great Dorset Steam Fair.

## The McCormick W-6

The W-6 was the standard-tread version of the Farmall M and was available with the same engine options. It was a favorite of farmers with medium to large acreage and limited row-crop cultivation. The W-6 was unsurpassed for belt work and was rated for three sixteen inch plows.

The O-6 Orchard was the same as the W-6 under the sweeping orchard fenders and driver's shield. Give this version two extra stars if the original fenders are in good condition. An OS-6 Orchard version was also available but differed little from the regular W-6. The headlights were mounted under the radiator, and the exhaust and air intakes were below the hood. There were some hood fairings but no orchard fenders. Nevertheless, the OS-6 rates an extra star.

There was also a Super W-6 version for which the torque amplifier option was available. The addition of the TA rates an extra star.

Rich and Roger Ramminger, of Morrisonville, Wisconsin, proudly show off their restoration work on this Farmall 400 at the 1993 Eagle River, Wisconsin, show. The man in the background with the hat is Mike Farrell, one of the show organizers.

Any shortcomings in the Farmall M were corrected in the Model 400. It was available in gasoline, LPG, or diesel models. A compression ratio increase on the nondiesel variants, plus breathing improvements boosted horsepower to over the 50 mark for the first time in a Farmall.

## The Farmall 400

As the replacement for the venerable M, the Farmall 400 was available in either gasoline, LPG, or diesel models. The same 264ci engine was used, but a compression ratio increase on the nondiesel variants plus breathing improvements boosted horsepower over the 50 mark for the first time in a Farmall, attaining parity with the John Deere 70. The 400 had a basic weight of about 5,600lb with-

The Super M had a 263.9ci engine with a bore and stroke of 4.00x5.25in. The long stroke resulted in a very flat torque curve. This allowed the Farmall to work as well with five transmission speeds as the competition did with six.

Even though the Super M was noted for its lugging ability, the torque amplifier was a welcome option in 1954. The TA gave a half step power shift down at the movement of a lever. This was generally enough to power through a tough spot.

out ballast.

Fast-Hitch and the torque amplifier were available, as was the live PTO. A special high-clearance version of the 400 was offered, which rates an extra star.

### The International W-400

The W-400 was essentially the same as the Farmall 400, except for the standard tread configuration. 15-30 rear tires were used instead of the 13-38 tires used on the Farmall. Also, instead of the over-the-engine steering, the W-400 used a more vertical steering shaft. The torque amplifier was featured, and both gasoline and diesel versions were available.

*Right*
Personal testimonies are featured in this Farmall ad from 1953. Note the claim of plowing twenty tough acres in an eight-hour day with a Super MD.

# "Even in tough plowing we turn 20 acres in an 8-hour day with our McCormick® Farmall® Super MD"

says A. C. Bradley,
Fulton County, Indiana

**"When we consider our Super MD's increased power,** fuel economy and faster field speeds, we really think we cut our plowing costs up to 40 percent," says Mr. Bradley. "We use only 15 to 20 gallons of fuel to plow 20 tough acres in an 8-hour day. Faster plowing rolls the dirt better, too— does a nicer job." Here is his son Bob, with the Farmall Super MD and 3-bottom McCormick plow.

"I've owned Farmalls 20 years, but my new Super MD—and its matching McCormick equipment—is the best yet. It helps me work fast . . . avoid delays . . . and it's more economical."

"I plowed up a road," reports Henry Longmeyer, Green County, Ill. "The ground was packed from hauling manure along the end of the field. We plowed it with the Farmall Super C and 2-furrow McCormick plow with Plow Chief bottoms. I liked the way the plow stayed in the ground. In tough ground, plowing 8 inches deep, the Super C goes five hours on a tank of fuel."

"Our Farmall Super M gives us plenty of power," says Walter Volk, Pierce County, N. D. "In one operation we plow 5 to 6 inches deep, work the soil, and drill up to 20 acres of wheat a day. The moist soil sprouts the seed fast— gives it a good start against weather hazards. IH equipment exactly fits our kind of farming. I couldn't farm as I do, without my Farmall Super M!"

**Prove that you, too, can save** while doing better, faster work with a Farmall tractor and matched McCormick equipment! There are five sizes of Farmall tractors in 10

The Super MD diesel demonstrated a maximum drawbar pull of 5,772lb during Nebraska testing in 1952. It weighed in for testing at 9,338lb.

Only about 4,000 W-400 tractors were built between 1955 and 1956.

### The Farmall 450

The Farmall 450 was built from 1956 to 1958 in regular and high-clearance versions (the latter gets an extra star). It was also available in diesel, gasoline, and LPG versions (the latter again gets an extra star). The engines received a displacement boost over that of the 400, to 281ci, making the 450 a true four-bot-tom tractor. Also, the fuel tank capacity was increased.

Approximately 40,000 Farmall 450s were delivered.

### The International W-450

This tractor related to the Farmall 450 just as the W-400 related to the Farmall 400. Only about 4,000 were built, however, which pushes them up to the five-star level without regard to the engine type.

Farmalls made in Germany had a D prefix, those made in Great Britain had a B prefix. The following letters and numbers did not necessarily follow the U.S. convention. This one appears to be a Super MD.

The Farmall Super M was built from 1952 through 1954. Its big 264ci four-cylinder engine gave it ample power (almost one-third more than the M). This one is owned by the Delbert Bunker Jr. family, who bought it new in 1952.

**Halt power take-off** for time-saving non-stop turns. Start pto whenever the tractor engine is running.

**Match travel speed to crop** and field conditions with TA, which gives two speeds in each gear. Just pull TA lever for instant speed change.

**Pto keeps running** at rated spee when you stop tractor travel. This mak it easy to clear heavy slugs.

# Change speed *on-the-go* with TA

## ...IH independent pto speed stays constant!

Now, harvest bunchy windrows and overgrown patches of crop without stops and shiftdowns! Torque Amplifier teamed with *completely* independent pto—on new Farmall® 350, 450, and International® 350 and W 450 tractors —give your pto-machines engine-drive performance! Just pull the TA lever to slow travel one-third—increase pull-power up to 45%—to save more crop in tough going. Through slow-downs and speed-ups, IH independent *pto holds rated speed.* You can stop pto any time . . . start it whenever tractor engine is running. Get *all* these engine-drive advantages without putting a $300 to $600 engine on your baler, combine, or chopper. *See your IH dealer for a speedier harvest at a big saving!*

See Your
### INTERNATIONAL HARVESTER Dealer

International Harvester products pay for themselves in use—McCormick Farm Equipment, Farmall and International Tractors . . . Motor Trucks . . . Construction Equipment . . . General Office, Chicago 1, Illinois.

**Big bunch but no slug!** A pull on the TA lever slows travel one-third while independent pto holds rated speed to help McCormick® No. 20-C field harvester "eat" right through big pile of hay—non-stop!

Advantages of the torque amplifier and live PTO are stressed in this 1957 ad.

Factory Cab? So claimed the sign accompanying this Farmall M at the 1994 Freeport, Illinois, show.

A close look at this Farmall 450 reveals an engine change from the original: this one has a GM 454ci V-8. It should have ample power for most jobs!

The M-TA was available with gasoline, diesel, and LPG fuels.

This beauty is owned by Austin G. Hurst, private-practice psychiatrist from Lafayette, California, who also has a Farmall 300 in similar condition. This 450 was restored by Dan Langy of Lena, Illinois.

# Chapter 5

# The Small Farmalls and Their Derivatives

| Rating | Model | Years Built |
|--------|-------|-------------|
| ★★ | F-12 | 1932-1938 |
| ★★★★★ | W-12 | 1932-1940 |
| ★★★ | F-14 | 1938-1939 |
| ★★★★★ | W-14 | 1938-1939 |
| ★★ | A | 1939-1953 |
| ★★★ | B | 1939-1947 |
| ★★★ | Super A | 1952-1954 |
| ★★ | C | 1948-1951 |
| ★★ | Super C | 1952-1954 |
| ★★★ | 100 | 1954-1956 |
| ★★★ | 130 | 1956-1958 |
| ★★★ | 200 | 1954-1956 |
| ★★★ | 230 | 1956-1958 |

*. . . there can be no such thing as
a good cheap tractor. . .*
Cyrus McCormick III, 1931,
*The Century of the Reaper*

## The Great Depression

The Great Depression that hit the United States and Canada in the fall of 1929, and the severe drought that accompanied it, brought many changes. Much of the once prosperous wheat-producing land of the Great Plains was abandoned. Farm income dropped worldwide, and with that came widespread unemployment in the manufacturing industry. Tractor production plummeted. In 1932, tractor sales in the United States dropped to around 19,000 units, down from the 200,000 mark set earlier in the decade—this was the lowest figure since 1915. Of the forty-seven tractor makers left after the Great Tractor War of the twenties, only seven of any substance remained producing wheel-type farm tractors in 1933. Ranked by size, they were:

1. International Harvester
2. Deere & Company
3. J.I. Case Company
4. Massey-Harris Company
5. Oliver Farm Equipment Company
6. Minneapolis-Moline Power Implement Company
7. Allis-Chalmers Company

The Farmall F-12 was a 15hp tractor introduced in 1932. It was available in either gasoline or kerosene versions and used a three-speed transmission.

By 1934, however, a 40 percent increase in tractor sales over 1933 made the survivors optimistic. Research and development continued unabated during this difficult period. Besides the continued trend toward row-crop configuration tractors, three other big changes occurred.

The first was the introduction of pneumatic tires. Around 1928, Florida citrus growers sought a solution to tree root damage caused by tractor cleats. They modified their steel rear wheels to mount discarded truck tire casings (without the inner tubes), sometimes placing as many as three casings side by side on each wheel. The casings were mounted in such a way that the natural strength in the curved rubber was enough to support the tractor without pneumatics. These "tires" provided both flotation and traction and proved so successful that the attention of the major tire companies was attracted. Within several years, pneumatic tires were available from several manufacturers. Allis-Chalmers was first to offer a tractor with such tires as standard equipment.

The second major development in the early thirties was in fuels. Kerosene had become the fuel of choice for agriculture since its use was pioneered by Hart-Parr. This was due, in part, to the great price disparity between kerosene and gasoline: kerosene was ten to fifteen cents cheaper per gallon than gasoline. However, the rise in acceptance of the automobile was forcing some rethinking of gasoline. As the primary automobile fuel, it was readily available, and some of its other advantages

The Farmall F-14 was built in 1938 and 1939. It was the successor to the F-12. The main difference was that its engine was rated at 1650rpm, rather than at 1400rpm, as was the F-12. This change gave the F-14 about 14 percent more horsepower. Note that the steering wheel is mounted higher on F-14s.

This 1938 Farmall F-14 was originally owned by the late Henry Smith of Ashton, Illinois. Collector Elwood Voss bought it, and it will soon be restored. Note the original Firestone rear tire on the left side (recognizable by its tread pattern).

The F-14 Farmall was available with either steel wheels or rubber tires and in dual narrow front, single front wheel, or wide front end arrangements. It was also available in gasoline (shown) and kerosene versions. Kerosene versions had a small gas tank embedded in the hood, providing gasoline for starting.

Both the F-12 and the F-14 could be equipped with a power lift. The operating mechanism is shown here.

This fancy original linkage clip has survived for more than fifty-six years on this F-14.

While many tractors relied on gravity to supply fuel to their carburetors, fuel pumps were used on F-12 and F-14 tractors.

Another difference between the F-12 and F-14: only F-14s had this valve cover breather.

Elwood Don Voss turns the crank on the F-14, while dad Elwood J. Voss looks on. When not working on their antique tractors, the Vosses farm 2,500 acres of corn and beans. Note the new Case International Magnum in the background. The Vosses trade in their big Case International combine every year.

began to outweigh the disadvantages of kerosene. With kerosene, fuel consumption was higher and less power was produced for a given displacement. Also, although not generally available for agriculture, by the early thirties, the first diesel tractors were on the market.

The third, and perhaps most profound change occurring in the early thirties, was the advent of the minitractor, designed to replace a team of horses. The hard economic times meant, for most farmers, that if a tractor was to be purchased it would have to be low cost.

Tractor manufacturers flooded the market with smaller, cheaper tractors, among them, the John Deere Model B, the Case RC, the Allis-Chalmers WC, and the small Farmall, the F-12.

### The Farmall F-12

The diminutive F-12 first appeared late in 1932. Although the asking price was around

This Farmall F-12 serves as a sign holder for the Happy Hill Farm near Fort Worth, Texas.

$550, only twenty-five were built that year. It was listed as a one-plow tractor, capable of pulling a 16in bottom. A PTO and fully adjustable rear wheel spacing were standard equipment.

The F-12 was originally equipped with a Waukesha engine, but soon one of Harvester's own designs was used. The 113ci engine was the same for both gasoline or kerosene fuel. Kerosene equipment consisted of a heated

This F-12 with factory wide-front is a rare find. This option originally added $45 to the price. Rubber tires added another $150 to the tractor's basic price of about $600.

Today's young farmers only shake their heads at the idea of check-row planting and cultivating. This F-12 is equipped with a wire-trip check row planter. It was being demonstrated at the 1994 Franklin Grove, Illinois, show.

Mounted implements for the F-12 Farmall are featured in this 1936 ad.

Production of the McCormick-Deering W-12 began in 1934 and ended in 1938. It was the standard-tread version of the F-12 row-crop Farmall. This one, owned by Ralph Oliver, Madrid, Iowa, was built in 1936.

Dan Schmitt of Omaha, Nebraska, maneuvers his McCormick-Deering O-12 (Orchard version of the F-12/W-12) at the 1994 Waukee, Iowa, show.

manifold and a separate gasoline tank for starting. For either fuel a 4.5:1 compression ratio was used and the rated operating speed was 1400rpm.

The early F-12s were equipped with a single front wheel. Later dual and wide-fronts were made available. The tractor could be adjusted to as narrow as 44.5in, the width of the standard horse. This made it ideal for the truck gardener, who was used to using one-horse specialized implements.

With its standard PTO, the F-12 could handle a 10ft binder or a 6ft mounted mower. The 7ft turning radius of the F-12 allowed for neat mowing in a square pattern. Front-mounted equipment included cultivators, hay sweeps, and side disk plows. A three-speed transmission was used for this 3,200lb tractor,

Since there were only about 4,000 W-12s made of all configurations, this I-12 is very rare.

The sweeping Orchard fenders of this O-12 dominate its profile. These fenders allowed the tractor to slip through the citrus groves without damaging the trees. Ralph Johnson of Waterman, Illinois, owns this example.

McCormick-Deering O-14s were only made in 1938 and 1939, and only a few were built each year, making the O-14 one of the most rare International Harvester tractors. Ralph Johnson, Waterman, Illinois, owns this one.

the F-12 was available on factory rubber from its first full year of production, which was 1933.

## The McCormick-Deering W-12

A standard-tread version of the F-12, the W-12, was essentially the same except for conversion to the lower, fixed-tread configuration. The W-12 was popular where row-crop cultivation was not required. The W-12 was also available as a Fairway version with special wheels for golf courses and airports, an I-12 Industrial version, and an O-12 Orchard version. Since only about 4,000 W-12s, 4,000 O-12s, 1,600 I-12s, and 600 Fairways were produced, all rate five stars.

## The Farmall F-14

Production of the F-12 ended with the 6,425th unit for 1938: more than 123,000 F-12s had been built since 1932. It was replaced by

the almost identical F-14. Production of the F-14 began in 1938 as soon as F-12 production ceased. The only visible difference was the identifying decal and the steering shaft angle. The difference was, however, that the engine was rated at 1650rpm rather than 1400rpm. This change gave the F-14 approximately 14 percent more horsepower, enough to handle two 14in plow bottoms. It was available in either gasoline- or kerosene-burning versions, and on either rubber or steel. Wheel weights were optional equipment when rubber tires were used.

The serial numbering system for the F-14 began with 124000 rather than beginning at Serial Number 501, as was usually the case for a new model. A gap of several hundred numbers was left after the last F-12.

Despite increasing competition, the F-14 sold well, with more than 27,000 units delivered in the two years of its production. Com-

As a plowing tractor, the W-12 was rated for one 16in bottom, or two twelves. Pretty good for such a small tractor. The W-12 was also noted for its ma-neuverability. This one belongs to Ralph Oliver of Madrid, Iowa, who is at the controls.

petition in 1938 included the Henry Dreyfuss-styled John Deere Model B and Model H. Allis-Chalmers came out with its nifty small Model B in 1938 and the narrow-front Model C in 1940, and Case had its Model R; all these were in the same power class as the F-14.

However, real competition came in June of 1939: Ford introduced the new 9N tractor, incorporating the Ferguson implement system. This 2,500lb tractor, selling for a mere $600, could plow more than twice as much acreage in a day as the $800 F-14. This unbe-lievable performance was made possible by the patented Ferguson System, the first vol-ume-production application of the hydraulic three-point hitch. With this system, the weight of any of a variety of implements, plus the draft and suction loads of the implement bore down on the rear wheels, greatly improving traction.

Time had caught up with the Farmall, indeed with the entire International Har-vester line. It was time for a complete mod-ernization.

Ike Martyn of Edgar, Wisconsin owns this Mc-Cormick-Deering I-12. He got it in Lathrop, Michigan, where it had worked for the county. When Ike acquired the tractor, it had a cracked block, four flat tires, and no hood.

### The McCormick-Deering W-14

The standard-tread version of the F-14 was the W-14. Again, there were Orchard, Fairway, and Industrial versions. 1,150 F-14s were built, along with 639 O-14s and 114 Fairway-14s. Estimates are that there were fewer than one hundred Industrial I-14s. All W-14 versions automatically rate five stars.

### The Farmall A

International Harvester was not caught napping by the competition. Seeing the trend toward more functional and eye-pleasing designs, Harvester engaged the services of Raymond Lowey, a noted industrial designer, who later gained worldwide renown with his design of the 1953 Studebaker car line. Lowey

104

The Farmall A used the same size engine as the F-12 and F-14, governed at 1400rpm. Its engine was offset to the left, and the operator seat and steering wheel were offset to the right. This gave the operator an unobstructed view of the ground beneath the tractor where the cultivator operated.

This is the 1939 Farmall A that was featured in the author's book *How To Restore Your Farm Tractor*. It was restored by Machinery Hill of Phillips, Wisconsin. After restoration, it was sold to Steve Williams of Ladysmith, Wisconsin, where it is now doing mowing duties. Rejuvenating an old small tractor, like this one, is still the cheapest way to get horsepower for serious yard work.

The Farmall B is essentially the same as the A. Model Bs do not look like Model As, however. The A has one long rear axle (on the right) and a short one on the left. The B has two long axles, left and right.

was commissioned to overhaul the entire IHC product line from the company logo to product operator ergonomics. By late 1938, the same year that John Deere brought out "styled" tractors, Harvester introduced the new TD-18 crawler tractor. The TD-18 was undeniably striking in its new, bright red, smoothly contoured sheet metal, hood, and grille. Just months later, a new line of wheel tractors was announced, continuing the styling motif and carrying it even further through the application of contoured fenders and styled wheels. The 1939 Lowey Farmalls look quite stylish, even today!

The first and most radical of these new tractors was the Farmall A. The A used the

A variation on the Model B theme: the Model BN. The BN has shorter rear axles.

same size engine as the F-12 and F-14, governed at 1400rpm. The most unusual feature was that the engine was offset to the left and the operator seat and steering wheel were offset to the right. This gave the operator an unobstructed view of the ground beneath the tractor where the cultivator would be operating. Lowey called this concept "Culti-Vision."

He reasoned that cultivating delicate crops was the major application of a tractor of this horsepower and so shaped everything around this task. With the offset engine the differential was close to the left rear wheel, and only the right had a proper axle. The right rear wheel required additional weight to give the A stability. The A was a utility-front machine. Nev-

The Farmall C replaced the Model B in 1948. The same 113.1ci engine was retained in both the gasoline and distillate configurations. The four-speed transmission was also retained.

ertheless, with its downward-extended king-pins, it retained the all-purpose functions for which Farmalls had become famous. It was equipped with both a belt pulley and a power take-off, but the belt pulley was in the back rather than at the side of the tractor.

The new A was available with either gasoline or kerosene engines, but as with all the "Lettered Series" tractors, gasoline predominated. The kerosene version used a compression ratio of 5:1 rather than 6:1, as on the gas engine. Thermo-siphon cooling was contin-

ued. Thermo-siphon is the label for liquid cooling systems that are generally not pressurized and that operate on the gravity principle, rather than employing a water pump. Late versions of the A did use a pump-type system, however, and many have been converted over the years. Also, with this system, radiator

*Right*
This 1953 ad for the Farmall Super C suggests ways to compare the Super C to competing tractors.

# Measure...Compare...Prove to yourself
## the McCormick Farmall® Super C
### is the Cultivating Champ of its class

*Here is the most practical way to buy a tractor:*

**Measure** the tractor in relation to your particular jobs.

**Compare** it, feature for feature, with any other tractor.

**Prove to yourself**—by actual operation on your own farm—that the Super C is unmatched in the all-purpose 2-row, 2-plow class.

**Measure** all your work. Compare the Super C and your choice of implements for each job, for quality, for top efficiency. Prove to yourself unmatched Super C job range.

**Measure** operating ease. Compare the hydraulic seat, the double-disc brakes, the handy controls. Prove to yourself you ride in comfort, drive with unmatched ease on a Super C.

**Measure** pull-power by socking a plow down deep in hard ground. Compare the surge of power. Prove to yourself that pound for pound the Super C has unmatched pull-power.

**Measure** economy. Compare first cost, upkeep, trade-in. Prove to yourself unmatched economy—15 to 25 percent more work on a gallon of gas on job after job.

**Measure** years of use. Compare normal service life, performance and durability. Prove to yourself by talking to any user, that Farmalls pay for themselves over and over.

The Farmall C was somewhat larger than the Model B it replaced, and it had the frame pads at the front for mounting implements such as cultivators.

shutters are used instead of a thermostat.

The A featured two wheel-brake pedals on the right side of the platform that could be actuated individually or locked together. A Donaldson oil-bath air cleaner was standard equipment, as was a high-tension magneto with an impulse coupling. A Delco-Remy generator and electrical system were optional. The system included lights and a starter. Rubber tires were standard, as was a four-speed transmission with a road gear giving a top speed of 10mph. A feature that made the Model A really useful was a power implement lift. Some early ones were pneumatic, but they soon went to hydraulic.

The Farmall AV was the identical tractor, with the exception of longer front kingpin extensions and 36x8in rear tires. This arrangement provided an additional 6in of clearance for crops such as asparagus and sugar cane. AV versions are worth two extra stars.

### The Farmall Super A

In 1947, a Super A version replaced the A. The Super A was identical to the A, except it had a built-in hydraulic system called "touch control." Most Super A tractors had 1650rpm engines, giving them a substantial power boost. Production of the Super A continued through 1954. A Super A-1 improved version with more hydraulic power was built toward the end of the production run. Give these an extra star.

### The Farmall B

The Farmall B was essentially the same tractor as the A, so much so that they were interspersed in the same serial numbering sequence. Model Bs do not look like Model As, however. The A has one long rear axle on the right and a short one on the left. The B has two long axles, left and right. Therefore, the engine of the B is in the middle, rather than offset to the left, as on the A. Nevertheless, the operator's seat is still offset to the right, and the steering column proceeds along the right side of the engine, as on the A.

All Model Bs had the "narrow front," with either a single or dual wheel, and were more after the tradition of the row-crop tractor than was the Model A. Rear wheels on both the A and B were reversible, to provide for row width changes of 28in. Both the A and B sold for about $600 in 1939, so were a direct challenge to the Ford-Ferguson 9N.

While the basic B weighed about a ton, ballast could be added, bringing the weight up

The Farmall A's main job as cultivating truck garden vegetables. The offset engine gave the operator an unobstructed view of the ground beneath the tractor. This concept was called Culti-Vision.

Rubber was standard for Farmall As and Bs, but this Model B has some interesting aftermarket steel rears.

Arlo Paxton of Stockton, Illinois, owns this Farmall B. The Model B was built between 1939 and 1947.

to almost two tons. Thus equipped, the B had little trouble with a 16in bottom pull-type plow. Other specialized implements included all those for the A, except those requiring hydraulic power, as the B was not built with internal hydraulics as was the Super A. Also, there were no Industrial or high-crop versions of the B.

### The Farmall C

The Farmall C more or less replaced the B in 1948. The same 113.1ci engine was retained in either the gasoline or distillate configuration. The four-speed transmission was also retained. The big difference between the A-B Series and the C was the inclusion in the C of a true operator's platform.

The Model C was fitted with hydraulic Touch Control. This was Harvester's first system for raising and lowering implements at the touch of a small lever. The Touch Control

system consisted of three elements: an engine-driven gear pump, a double work cylinder, and a valve unit. Two rockshafts operated four rockshaft power arms to separately control left and right implements. In 1950, Harvester unveiled a marketing program where a number of Farmall Cs were delivered to dealers in a white paint scheme. Many of these survive today and are much sought after by collectors. Evidence of originality garners one of these white Farmalls a five-star rating.

### The Super C

The Super C replaced the C in 1951. The big feature of the Super C was an increase in engine displacement from 113.1 to 122.7ci. Displacement was increased through 1/8in increase in bore diameter, giving the Super C a 15 percent increase in horsepower. The Super C was rated as a 14in bottom two-plow tractor.

Additionally, the Super C had other interesting new features: a new ball-ramp disk brake system and an upholstered seat with an adjustable double-acting shock absorber with a conical coil spring. The hydraulic Touch Control was now standard rather than optional.

The Super C was available in either dual tricycle or adjustable wide-front configurations. The C and the Super C can be readily distinguished from their stablemates by the high steering wheel position and the sharp angle of the steering shaft as it proceeds past the left side of the cowling.

## The Farmall 100

The Farmall 100 and its stablemate, the Industrial I-100, were built from 1954 to 1956 in regular and high-clearance models (give the high-clearance version an extra star). Styling was continued in the all-red theme with the insignia now in chrome letters. The Farmall 100 was essentially the same as the Super A, except the engine displacement was increased from 113ci to 123ci, and the compression ratio was increased from 6:1 to 6.5:1. The rated speed was dropped from 1650rpm to 1400rpm. Although the Super A was not test-

Henry Ford and the 1939 9N Ford-Ferguson tractor, the tractor that revolutionized the tractor world with the load-compensating three-point hitch. The occasion of this photo was the press introduction in June of 1939. After plowing demonstrations by Ford and Harry Ferguson, both experienced plowmen, the eight-year-old boy shown looking at Ford then mounted the tractor and plowed furrows that were just as good.

Replacing the Model 200, the Farmall 230 was introduced in 1956. It used the 123ci gasoline four-cylinder engine governed at 1800rpm. The 230 was a nominal 28hp machine.

ed at Nebraska, it is estimated that these changes canceled each other out. Nevertheless, the 100 was rated for one 14in plow or two 12in plows. Steering, brakes, and powertrain were also somewhat beefed up.

The biggest improvement in the Model 100 was the International Harvester Fast-Hitch coupled to the Touch Control hydraulics. Fast-Hitch was IH's answer to the Ford-Ferguson three-point hitch. Its advantage was that the operator could merely back into the imple-

ment and pick it up with no need to dismount to insert pins or latch latches.

### The Farmall 130

The Farmall 130 and industrial International I-130 tractors were produced between 1956 and 1958. The Model 130 was the same as the Model 100 except for the white grille and side panels and the 1650rpm-rated engine speed, which made it a nominal 20hp tractor. An HV (high clearance) version was available and rates two extra stars.

### The Farmall 200

The Farmall Super C, which the 200 replaced, already had the 123ci engine operating at 1650rpm. The 200 got the compression ratio increase from 6:1 to 6.5:1, and therefore registered a little more horsepower in the Nebraska tests. Otherwise, it was the same as the Super C, except for changes to the grille and nameplates.

### The Farmall 230

This was the 1956-1958 version of the Farmall C. The engine speed was upped to 1800rpm for this edition, putting it in the over 25hp class.

# Chapter 6

# The Big Standards

| Rating | Model | Years Built |
|--------|-------|-------------|
| ★★★ | W-40 | 1934-1940 |
| ★★★★ | WD-40 | 1934-1940 |
| ★★★★★ | I-40 | 1934-1940 |
| ★★★★★ | ID-40 | 1934-1940 |
| ★★ | W-9 | 1940-1953 |
| ★★★★ | I-9 | 1940-1953 |
| ★★ | WD-9 | 1945-1953 |
| ★★★★ | ID-9 | 1945-1953 |
| ★★★★ | Super WDR-9 | 1953-1956 |
| ★★★★ | Super WR-9S | 1953-1956 |
| ★★★★ | Super WD-9S | 1953-1956 |
| ★★★★ | 600 | 1956 |
| ★★★ | 650 | 1956-1958 |
| ★★ | 660 | 1959-1963 |

*Henry Ford had the time, money and inclination to poke sticks at the McCormicks. He loved to, we've heard from the horses mouth.*
Elmer Baker Jr., Staff Writer,
*Implement and Tractor Magazine,* 1925

## Origins of the Standard Tractor

A standard-tread tractor is one that has a fixed-tread width. At least that's how it started out. The tread width of most standard-treads from the thirties and forties could be changed by reversing the wheels or by changing the wheel-rim relationship.

Nevertheless, the term standard-tread has come to mean a tractor that is not a row-crop machine. Row-crops generally had a splined-axle with adjustable rear treads and either a narrow front or an adjustable front axle.

In addition, standard-tread tractors were built lower to the ground for a lower center of gravity. This provided greater stability, especially with a sideways pull.

The original internal combustion tractor was created by mounting a gasoline engine on a steam engine chassis. Such was the case with the 1892 Froelich, the first internal combustion tractor able to propel itself both backward and forward. It is only natural that early tractors would resemble the steamers from which they were developed.

By the mid-twenties, the automobile had become popular enough to have taken on a conventional configuration. This included the radiator, engine, driver's position, and cab. Some of the tractors of this period adopted elements of this configuration. In 1917, International Harvester came out with the International 8-16 tractor, which was based on the Model G truck. In fact, it looked like a fore-shortened truck.

Ford had entered the truck business in 1917, a province originated by Harvester, and was consistently rumored to also be readying a Model T-like tractor. Ford's low-cost haulers were soon smothering the market, and it was feared that his tractors would do the same.

Late in 1917, Ford started building his long-awaited low-cost tractor, soon known as the Fordson. By 1920, the Fordson had knocked Harvester from the number one position on the sales chart. International Harvester's reaction to Ford was to quickly design two Fordson look-alikes: the 15-30 and the 10-20. The intense competition of the 1920s encouraged the other tractor makers to bring out tractors with similar configurations, and these became the "standards." They were squat and low; most used the engine, transmission, and differential castings as the frame; the radiator was in front; and a trucklike hood was used to

The W-9 was a big standard tractor with operating weights around 11,000lb. Its engine was a 335ci four-cylinder unit, with a rated speed of 1500rpm. Bore and stroke were 4.4x5.5 . It was originally available in gasoline or distillate versions. Later a diesel was added.

cover the engine back to a trucklike cowling. The driver sat behind the rear wheels where the controls of pulled implements could be reached.

The standards became popular in wheat country, where tractor cultivation of row crops was not a requirement. The nature of the large-acreage wheat farm led to larger and larger standard-tread machines and to the names "Wheatland" and "Western" for some of them.

### The McCormick-Deering W-40

Besides the 15-30 and 10-20 tractors, McCormick-Deering built standard-tread versions of their popular row-crop tractors. These were the W-12, W-14, W-4, W-30, and W-6. The first of the big McCormick-Deering Wheatlands, however, was the W-40, which

was brought out in 1934. It featured a six-cylinder engine of the same type as that used in International heavy-duty trucks. The engine had also been used in the McCormick-Deering T-35 and T-40 TracTracTor crawler beginning in 1932 and was available in different displacements of 279 and 298ci.

There were two serial number prefixes for W-40s: WAC and WKC. WAC indicated the 279ci engine was used, while WKC was used for the 298ci engine.

The bore and stroke for the W-40 was 3.75x4.5in for a piston displacement of 298ci. The engine was rated at two rotational speeds: 1600rpm and 1750rpm. Separate Nebraska tests (Numbers 268 and 269) were conducted at each rated speed.

Technically, the correct designation was WK-40, as this tractor operated on kerosene. It

The WD-9 had the same engine as the W-9 but beefed up to handle the diesel loads. It also had the Harvester gasoline starting system. The WD-9 was based on the big TD-9 crawler.

This WD-9 is making short work of a pile of logs at the 1993 Eagle River, Wisconsin, show. Steady belt power was one of the main features of these big standards.

This WD-9 is powering a sawmill at the 1993 Eagle River, Wisconsin, show. The WD-9 developed just under 50 horsepower, about the same as the gasoline W-9.

The International Model 600 was only built in 1956. It was essentially the same tractor as the W-9, but was redesignated to be parallel with the other numbered Harvester tractors.

was a big tractor, weighing in at around 7,600lb. At 1600rpm, the maximum belt horsepower was listed at 43, while at the 1750rpm setting, maximum belt horsepower was 49, a respectable number for a wheeled tractor of this period. The diesel WD-40 was the first variation on the W-40 theme. It was also the first diesel wheel tractor. When the WD-40 was introduced in 1934, the country's first diesel tractor, the Caterpillar Diesel 65, had only been in existence since 1931.

The WD-40 had an entirely different engine from the W-40. For the WD-40, four, rather than six cylinders were used. The bore and stroke were 4.75x6.5, giving a displacement of 471ci.

Although the diesel WD-40 cost one and one half times as much as a gasoline W-40, most farmers found it well worth the investment—it used about a third less fuel than the W-40.

The IK-40 and ID-40 were essentially the same as the W-40 and WD-40 but with a standard pintle hitch and an "armchair" seat. Most of the I versions were equipped with truck-type dual rear wheels but did not come with fenders. Only about one hundred I-40s and only about 240 of the ID-40s were built.

## The McCormick-Deering W-9

The W-9 was based on the big T-9 crawler. The engine was a 335ci four-cylinder unit, with a rated speed of 1500rpm. Bore and stroke were 4.4x5.5in. It was originally available in gasoline or distillate versions; add a star for the distillate version.

Nebraska tests indicated a maximum horsepower for the gasoline W-9 at 49, while the distillate burner produced 45. The standard rear tires for the W-9 were 13.50-32 (early) and 14-34 (late) with 7.50-18s in the front. The W-9 had a shipping weight of about 6,400lb.

The diesel version, the WD-9, was of the same basic design and used the same size engine, but the engine was beefed up to handle diesel loads. The WD-9 developed about the same horsepower as the gasoline W-9. The diesel versions also used a twelve-volt electrical system with two six-volt batteries. WD-9s weighed about 800lb more than the W-9. Typical operating weights with ballast for both ran about 11,000lb.

With production starting in 1945, the I-9 and ID-9 were virtually the same tractors, except for the heavy cast rear wheels and the use of 13-32 tires. These were great loader tractors.

The International 600 was also available in a diesel version, as shown here. This 600D, owned by Don Corrie, is the first one made.

This International 650LP is owned and operated by Don Corrie. The International 650 was a redesignation of the previous Model 600. Besides the LPG version shown here, there were also diesel and gasoline options.

Don Corrie's International 650LPG as seen at the 1994 Sandwich, Illinois, show. The 650's engine displaced 350ci and produced about 65hp. A five-speed transmission was used.

Another variation of the W-9 was the WR-9, the rice field version. It was also available as the WRD-9. The primary difference was in the use of special rice tires in sizes of 15-34, or 18-26 as singles, or in 14-32 as duals. Surprisingly, steel wheels remained an option. Special wide fenders were also supplied equipped with rice shields in front to protect the platform. Other features of the rice tractors included a hand clutch and a foot "decelerator" to override the governor when traversing bumps. The Rice Specials are five-star collector tractors.

In 1953, "Super" was added to the designation of International Harvester tractors. The WD-9 became the Super WD-9, the WR-9 became the Super WR-9S, and the WDR-9 became the Super WDR-9. There were no Super W-9s or industrials. For the Supers, the dis-

This view shows the roomy platform of Don Corrie's immaculate 650LP. Notice the free-standing instrument panel.

This International M-R-S Special, in fresh Army Olive paint, made an appearance at the 1994 Waukee, Iowa, show.

placement was upped to 350ci. Maximum horsepower was 65, putting it in the same class as the John Deere 80 and the Case 500.

### The International 600

The 600 was unique among the big wheatland tractors as it was built only in 1956. It was essentially the same tractor as the WD-9 but was redesignated to be parallel with the other numbered Harvester tractors. It was a full five-plow machine and was available as either a gasoline or diesel model. A few industrial models were also built. They rate an extra star.

### The International 650

Again, the International 650 was merely a redesignation of the previous 600. Besides the diesel and gasoline versions, there was now an LPG version. The five-speed transmission was retained. As with the 600, a few industrials were built and rate an extra star, as does

The International 660 was available in gasoline, diesel, and LPG versions. The gasoline and LPG engines displaced 263ci, while the diesel was 281ci. All were six-cylinder engines. It was built between 1959 and 1963. The International 660, which replaced the 650, was in the 80hp class.

The Model 600D was only built in 1956. It was International Harvester's answer to the John Deere Model R and the later Model 80. Or possibly these Deere tractors were built to compete with the successful IH WD-9, which was the forerunner of the Model 600D.

the LPG version. Therefore, an industrial LPG 650 would rate five stars.

## The International 660

The Model 660, introduced in 1959, was a considerable upgrade from the 650. It was completely restyled, following the theme of the rest of the Harvester tractor line, which was restyled in 1958. A torque amplifier power shift was available, giving the 660 ten speeds forward and two in reverse. The big change was in the engine, however. A smaller six-cylinder unit was used, with 263ci for gasoline and LPG versions, and 281ci for the diesel. These engines were high-speed types, rated at 2400rpm. Therefore, they produced more power than their predecessors. The engines developed about 80hp, putting them in the same class as the Oliver 990 GM and the Minneapolis-Moline GVI.

Give an extra star to the gasoline and LPG versions of the 660.

# Chapter 7

# The Cub

| Rating | Name | Model Year |
|--------|------|------------|
| ★★★ | Farmall Cub | 1947-1950 |
| ★★ | Farmall Cub | 1950-1958 |
| ★★ | International Cub | 1958-1975 |
| ★★★ | International Cub Lo-Boy | 1955-1975 |

*No Weapon is too small for a brave man.*
Old Proverb

Introduced in 1947, the Cub was of the same Culti-Vision configuration as the Farmall A. Cultivation of delicate plants was to be its priority job, and as originally configured, the Cub weighed only 1,500lb.

The Cub was born in the difficult post-World War II years. By 1947, most tractor makers had their postwar designs out, and all could see that it was to be a time for the survival of the fittest. At first, they had not appreciated the competition brought about by the Ford-Ferguson 9N and the three-point hitch, but the 9N had gained market share all through the war. By 1947, not only was there an improved version, the 8N, but when Ford

The rear-engined Allis-Chalmers Model G was also in the Farmall Cub's power class.

Many custom implements were available for the Farmall Cub. Shown here is a unique one-arm loader. The Cub had a 69in wheelbase and an adjustable width from 40 to 56in.

and Ferguson finally split in July of 1947, Ferguson began importing his look-alike British TE-20 to supply his considerable dealer network.

International Harvester's response was improvements to their entire line, plus the introduction of a new, smaller, less-expensive tractor, the Farmall Cub. The theory was that there would be a Farmall tailored for every application, thereby overwhelming the single-model Ford.

The Cub was aimed at the market of the John Deere H, L, and LA. Their market was that of the vegetable grower, nursery operator, landscaper, and the small-acreage farmer still using only a team of draft animals. Interestingly, John Deere dropped out of this market in 1947, by replacing the small L and LA models with the Model M, which was designed to attack Ford head-on.

Separately, it is difficult to tell a Cub from a Farmall A. Together, the Cub looks like a scale model of the A. The most distinguishing visual feature of the Cub is the shape of the gas tank, which is rounded, rather than tear drop-shaped on the other Farmalls.

The 1,500lb Cub used a unique little 59.5ci four-cylinder engine. It is unique in that it is a side-valve engine (L-head), rather than the valve-in-head type used by the other Farmalls. This 10hp unit found other applications as a power unit for combines, pumps, blowers, and so on. In the 1950 version, operating speed of the engine was raised from 1600 to

Here is a Farmall Cub from the late fifties painted highway yellow. It is equipped with a belly-mounted rotary mower. The Cub used a 59.5ci four-cylinder L-head engine of about 12hp.

This bright yellow Cub appeared to have just been painted when it was seen at the 1994 Waukee, Iowa, show. The Cub was dwarfed by the big Oil-Pulls behind it.

1800rpm, giving the Cub approximately 10 percent more power.

The Cub lived and died with a three-speed transmission, a unit that somewhat limited its capabilities. First gear provided a speed of a little over 2mph and third gave a top speed of about 6.5mph. Other tractors in the Cub's power class were the Massey Pony and the rear-engined Allis-Chalmers Model G.

The Cub had a 69in wheelbase and an adjustable width of 40 to 56in.

An interesting variation was the Cub Lo-Boy. This model sat considerably lower than other Cub models. Its stance was 7in lower, and it had an underneath exhaust, as opposed to the above-the-hood exhausts on other Cubs. The Lo-Boy was ideal for estate and golf course mowing with a belly-mounted mower. Most Lo-Boys were labeled "International,"

Lee Huber of Jefferson, Wisconsin, proudly shows off his freshly restored 1948 Farmall Cub. It was difficult to tell the difference between the sound the Cub was making and that of a well-oiled electric motor.

A 1956 International Cub Lo-Boy, with owner Jon Kayser, Dell Rapids, South Dakota, aboard. The later Cubs were not Farmalls, but rather Internationals.

but a few had the "Farmall" title. After 1958, all Cubs were Internationals.

Originally, Cubs had seven or eight custom implements built for them. Later, that number doubled and included a one-armed front-end loader, as the little tractor found more and more uses. The tractor was equipped with magneto ignition, but an electrical system (starter and lights) was available. Also available as optional equipment were a rear PTO and Touch Control hydraulics. The Cub and its variations continued in Harvester's inventory into the 1970s, although they were much improved in 1970.

The author's son, Greg Pripps, stands by Jon Kayser's 1948 Farmall Cub. Like the Farmall A, its engine was offset to the left with the driver and steering wheel to the right.

# Chapter 8

# Farmalls in Final Form

| Rating | Model | Years Built |
|--------|-------|-------------|
| ★★ | 140 | 1958-1979 |
| ★★★ | 240 | 1958-1962 |
| ★★★ | 330 | 1957-1958 |
| ★★ | 340 | 1958-1963 |
| ★★ | 460 | 1958-1963 |
| ★★ | 560 | 1958-1963 |

*The Farmall is the greatest machine developed
for farmers since the reaper.*
From a 1929 customer letter to IH

As the decade of the fifties came to an end, styling, safety, and comfort became big selling features for tractors. Diesel engines were gaining prominence and LPG fuel held its own as distillate had all but disappeared. The trend in tractor configuration was clearly toward the utility front end. Power shift torque amplifier transmissions were the norm for the larger tractors and some were using torque converters ahead of their manual transmissions. Ford had introduced its Select-O-Speed ten-speed power shift. Tractors that

An International 300 Utility, for sale along the road in northwestern Wisconsin. International Model 300s, 330s, and 350s were essentially the same, except for trim.

This International 350 Utility is owned by Roland Spude of Dykesville, Wisconsin. He says it has spent a good part of its life logging. It is equipped with a Henry Manufacturing Company loader, from Topeka, Kansas. Spude says it's a good working tractor, but that much weight has to be carried on the rear lift to counteract the weight in the bucket. This is because the front wheels are located so far back.

used loaders were being equipped with shuttle shifts to permit backward and forward movement in each transmission gear by moving the shuttle lever.

At the end of the decade, there were still seven major tractor companies in the Western Hemisphere: John Deere, International Harvester, Case, Ford, Oliver, Allis-Chalmers, and Massey-Ferguson. All were scrambling for a share of the market.

In 1958 the entire International Harvester line of tractors was restyled focusing on a new, more forceful-appearing grille. The larger models were completely new, while the lower end counted on the face-lift to remain competitive.

### The Farmall/International 140

The 140 was the last in the Culti-Vision line of small tractors. It was essentially the same as the previous Model 130, except for the new styling. In fact, the 140 retained most of the characteristics of the Farmall A from 1939, making it a contender with the John

Duane Helman's International 300 Utility tractor with a Holdren Bros. (West Liberty, Ohio) high-lift loader. The driver's seat and controls are on the right side of the engine, facing aft. A cherry-picker bucket is currently installed. Duane is president and founder of Rosewood Machine and Tool Company, Rosewood, Ohio, and is himself a tractor collector. His company manufactures a catalog full of reproduction hard-to-get parts for old tractors.

This International 240 Utility is at work for a landscaper. The 240 U and the Farmall 240 were successors to the Model C.

The instrument panel of the International 240 U.
The 240 was made from 1958 to 1962.

Deere D as the longest-produced model at thirty years (the original worm-drive Fordson survived for twenty-nine years).

The 140 retained the 123ci engine and the four-speed transmission. High-clearance and International industrial models were also available. These two rate one extra collector star apiece.

### The Farmall/International 240

The 240 featured the same 123ci four-cylinder engine used in the 140. The difference was that it was rated at 2000rpm in the 240, rather than the 1400rpm of the 140. However, the tractor was a complete redesign of the old 230, now with on-center steering replacing the shaft alongside the engine that began with the Farmall C. The

weight of the 240 was just under 4,000lb, although the weight could exceed 6,000lb in working trim. The four-speed transmission of the previous models was retained.

The Farmall 240 had a dual narrow front end and was available in a high-clearance version, which rates an extra star. The International 240 was a utility tractor with a lower stance and an adjustable wide front end. Production of the Farmall version ended in 1961 while the International version continued through 1962.

### The International 330

The Model 330 was only built as an International, and only in the utility configuration. Also, its production run lasted only through 1957 and 1958. The 330 used the 135ci engine

This International 240 U is equipped with the Fast-Hitch.

from the T-340 crawler, which had a maximum horsepower of 32.

The 330 used a five-speed transmission with the torque amplifier power shift underdrive. The rear tires were size 12-28, while the fronts were 5.5-16. The weight of this tractor was about 4,500lb, but it could be ballasted to as much as 6,500lb.

The 330 made a great loader tractor. It was normally equipped with the Fast-Hitch, and its short wheelbase made it maneuverable in tight quarters.

### The Farmall/International 340

The 340 was a completely new tractor, and was available either in the International utility version, or as a Farmall row-crop with either adjustable wide or narrow front ends. The engine was the same 32hp 135ci four-cylinder unit used in the Model 330. The

International Harvester collector Larry Johnson with his 1959 International 340 Utility. This tractor used the 135ci four-cylinder engine. It was in the 35hp class.

This 1961 Farmall 560 is equipped with the Elwood Front Wheel Drive System. This was a retrofit system, which, according to the advertising, could be removed and returned to the original configuration in about an hour. This one is owned by Wilbur Marshall of Earlville, Illinois.

torque amplifier power shift underdrive transmission was an option to the five-speed transmission. Also available was a choice of two- or three-point Fast-Hitch with Traction-Control and Tel-A-Depth, Harvester's version of Ferguson's draft control.

It weighed a little under 5,000lb, but another 2,000lb of ballast could be added. Thus equipped, the 340 was an honest three-plow tractor. These were modern and capable tractors in their day and today they make great collector tractors.

## Farmall/International 460

The 460 was available in the low-profile International utility version and the regular Farmall row-crop type. The Farmall was also available as a high-clearance model, which

The Farmall 560 was available in gasoline, LPG, and diesel versions. The gasoline and LPG engines displaced 263ci, while the diesel version displaced 281ci, and all versions had six cylinders. These engines put the 560 in the 60hp class and gave it a full five-plow rating.

gave an extra 12in of crop clearance.

Three engine types were available: diesel, LPG, or gasoline. The LPG and gasoline versions were 221ci while the diesel displaced 236ci. All were six-cylinder powerplants and all delivered a little over 50hp, making the 460 a four-plow machine. All versions of the 460 used a five-speed transmission with the torque amplifier available. Competitive tractors in the 460's class were the Oliver 770, the Case 800, and the John Deer 630.

Give an extra collector star to the LPG version and another one for the high-clearance version. Thus a high-clearance LPG Model 460 would rate four stars.

## The Farmall 560

One of the best selling and most popular tractors of its time, the big 560 was the top of

The Farmall 460 was the first six-cylinder Farmall. It was available in 221ci–gasoline and LPG versions, or with a 236ci diesel. It was also available in the International Utility configuration in gasoline and diesel versions. The 460 was about a 50hp tractor.

The Model 340 replaced the 330 in 1958. It was available in the Farmall or International Utility configurations. Shown here is the Farmall with adjustable wide front.

1958 International 240 Utility. The 240 was also available as the Farmall 240. Both used the 123ci gasoline engine and the four-speed transmission. The 240 replaced the Model 230 and was in the 30hp class.

The International 330 was only made in the Utility configuration, and only in the years 1957 and 1958. The 135ci gasoline four-cylinder engine was used.

The Farmall 140 was the successor to the great original Farmall A. The same Culti-Vision configuration was used, as was the 123ci gasoline engine.

Engine operating speed was still 1400rpm, but horsepower was now over 20 due to increased compression ratio and breathing improvements.

the Farmall line. Its six-cylinder engine was available for gasoline, LPG, and diesel. All produced about 60hp, giving the 560 a five-plow rating. In working trim, the 560 weighed in at about 10,000lb, putting it in the same class as the John Deere 730 and the Cockshutt 570.

The 560's diesel engine displaced 282ci, while the gasoline and LPG versions had 263ci. These were the same engines used in the big 660 standard-tread tractor. Give an extra collector star to a 560 with the LPG engine.

# Chapter 9

# Buying and Keeping a Collector Tractor

*Put yourself in the position of the police officer who investigates the theft of an antique tractor...*
Craig Beek, Manager, Corporate Security,
Deere & Company

There are as many reasons for collecting and restoring old tractors as there are old tractor collectors. For some, it's nostalgia, a regard for the old days when life was simpler (and Dad paid the bills), and brand loyalty was strong. For others its an appreciation for fine old machinery and the craftsmanship displayed in a first-rate restoration. For others, there is just the need for some horsepower around the place, and a restored old tractor is usually cheaper than a new one. This last reason is often used by today's farmer who needs an extra loader tractor, or one just to provide PTO power for an auger or a pump.

For whatever reason, tractor collecting and restoring is booming. The experienced farmer can usually pick out a good tractor from the poor tractors at a considerable distance, but this chapter is for those who can't.

Besides the star rating system given in the introduction, there is another type of rating system, the "class system," used by antique and collectible car and tractor people to define the condition and state of restoration of their vehicles. This system is especially helpful in over-the-phone dealings, or in collector magazine sales advertisements:

### Class 1: Excellent

Class 1 tractors have been restored to current professional standards in every area or are completely original. All components operate like new. In all appearances these tractors are brand new and unused. In other words, "Concours Condition."

### Class 2: Fine

Tractors categorized as class 2 include well-restored or superior restorations, along with excellent originals, or extremely well-maintained originals, showing minimal wear.

### Class 3: Very Good

The class 3 rating is used for a completely operable original tractor, an older restoration now showing wear, or an amateur restoration not quite up to professional standards. It is presentable and serviceable inside and out, but not a class 1 or 2. Also in this class are good partial restorations with parts to complete, and other variations on the theme.

### Class 4: Good

Class 4 tractors are operable or need minor work to become operable. Also included are deteriorated or poorly accomplished restorations and those in need of complete restoration. Generally, a class 4 tractor is one that is, or has recently been, used for work and has not been refurbished.

## Class 5: Restorable

Tractors rated class 5 need complete restoration. They may or may not be drivable, but are not weathered, wrecked, or stripped to the point of being useful only for salvage.

Be aware that there are two definite approaches to restoring old tractors: restoring to original or refurbishing to serviceable. Any tractor with a three-star or higher rating should be restored, and the class system presumes that such is the case. It is a travesty to carelessly refurbish, rather than restore, a valuable antique. Even with one- and two-star tractors, consideration should be given before originality is sacrificed. Assume that someday you, or someone else, may want to return the tractor to its original state. Examples are conversion to a twelve-volt electrical system or cutting off the steel rims to substitute rubber tires.

If you already have your tractor, then you won't have to face the choosing and buying problems. If, however, you don't already have one but have decided which model you want and the level of restoration you are prepared to handle, then the acquisition phase is next. The handy checklist included in this chapter will help you organize your thoughts and will also help you arrive at a fair price for the tractor.

Perhaps the first decision you should make is the level of restoration you want. Are you interested in a 100 percent original restoration? Do you just want to have a nice old tractor around to help you with gardening and making firewood? Or are you somewhere in between? You must understand that those who are into originality go all the way! Originality means not using modern-tread tires. It means using wiring, hose clamps, spark plugs, and tire valve caps from the tractor's era. It means being a stickler for details that most people wouldn't notice. This level of restoration is essential to realize the potential value of a four- or five-star tractor. If you have a run-of-the-mill tractor, then maybe something less than original will be sufficient. The sad part of this is that a true five-star machine is not good for anything but display and an occasional parade. I find that people with such tractors always have at least one of lesser value around for work and fun.

Next, you need to decide whether you want to buy an already restored tractor or one you can restore completely by yourself. A third option is to do some of the work and then get some expert help. Whichever course you take it is essential that your objectives for both class rating and cost are clearly defined.

Where do you look for a collectible International-built tractor? The first place for a 1939, or later, tractor is the farm equipment section of your local newspaper. Your local International tractor dealer is usually a good source. Often, the dealer will have an H or a 230 on the used tractor row. For the old International, or anything unusual, try other collectors or an ad placed in the *IH Collector's Newsletter* or *Red Power Magazine*. You can also check the antique tractor line-up at your local thresheree and steam show.

The search for the tractor you want can be an emotional experience. Your hopes might be dashed if your expectations are too high. Looking for a class 3 but secretly hoping for a class 5 can be disappointing. But don't be discouraged. Just be realistic. Remember, the important questions are: is the price fair, and do you want to get involved in the amount of work required to put the tractor into the shape you want? To help you determine the fairness of the price and to systematically determine how much work and cost you would be facing, the following buyer's checklist is included. For best results, customize it for the type of tractor you are looking for and for the type of work you are willing to undertake.

Make copies of this checklist and take one with you when you go to evaluate a tractor for purchase. Check the items off as they appear on the list, making notes on each section as you go. The purpose of this is twofold: first, it's an orderly way to complete the evaluation with as much rationality as possible, and second, it gives you a good record of the evaluation for comparison to others you find, thereby getting a handle on the fairness of the price. If you are going to hire some or all the work out, your notes on the checklist will help your mechanic give you a cost estimate. The checklist will be followed by explanations of the items and what to look for.

## General Checklist

### General Appearance
Sheet metal / grill /fenders
Tires /wheels
Steering wheel condition
Gauges: correct /operable
Seat: correct /condition
Exhaust
Oil leaks / water leaks /fuel leaks
Model designation
Serial number
Ask what is included (wheel weights, implements, etc.)

### Steering
Steering wheel free play
Kingpin free play
Radius rod free play
Front wheel bearing free play
Drag arm(s) free play

## Before Starting

### Engine
Water pump or generator shaft end play
Belt pulley end play
Evidence of crack repair, block /head
Oil in crankcase
Filter in place
Water in crankcase
Water in radiator
Oil in water
Belts
Hoses
Radiator cap
Air cleaner
Carburetor /injector controls
Fuel tank /fuel in tank
Fuel filter sediment bowl/shut-off turned on

### Electrical
Battery in place /condition /water
Battery box corrosion
Magneto
Cables /terminals
Generator brushes
Starter: visible condition
Key/switch: location /operation
Diesel shut-off operational
Ammeter indication: key on and off

Plug wire condition
General wiring condition
Lights

### Clutch/Transmission
Clutch operation
Shift lever operation
Oil level
Water in oil
Leaks /welds /repairs
Shift lever boot (if so equipped)

### Rear Axle
Housing cracks /repairs / leaks
Lubricant level /water present?
Axle wheel seals
Brakes / lining / linkage

## After Starting

### Engine
Oil pressure
Smoke: tailpipe /breather
Knocking
Missing
Temperature stabilizes
Throttle response rpm range /governor operation
Oil leaks /water leaks /hydraulics leaks
Starter operation
Generator charging

### Clutch/Transmission
Clutch releases completely
Gear selection
Clutch engages smoothly
Clutch slippage
Free pedal
PTO operation
Differential lock operation

### Brakes
Left and right brake power

### Hydraulic System
Lift ability
Leak down
Smoothness

### Road /Field Test
Steering shimmy /binding

Brakes
Engine operation under load
Hydraulics operation
Water temperature
Inappropriate noises

## Comments to the General Checklist
### Before Starting:

It is important that these tests are done before attempting to start the engine, unless the tractor has been recently run. Not only will this prevent damage from things like lack of oil, but it will allow you to check for water in the oil, or oil in the water, before operation gets everything mixed up. It will, in addition, serve as a setup check so you don't, for example, attempt to start the engine with the fuel shut off.

## General Appearance

Rust and corrosion indicate long periods of outdoor storage. This can ruin internal parts as well as the external. Look for extraneous holes or modifications to the sheet metal and fenders. If these parts are not repairable, some of them can be expensive to replace. Check for proper sheet metal fasteners. If you are going for a four- or five-star restoration, visible fasteners must be the original type. If the paint job is recent, is it good enough for you, and are the decals proper? If not, you will be asked to pay for something you can't use.

## Model Designation and Serial Number

These are included so that proper credit will be given if the tractor is historically significant or rare. Lack of definite evidence of model or serial number can impede the acquisition of parts and may be evidence that the configuration is not original.

## Tires and Wheels

Do they match, left and right? Are the tires weather checked? Hairline cracks are acceptable, but major cracks will cause trouble. Splits and cracks can indicate the existence of a boot or tire liner. These are OK, but reduce the value. A new set of current-production tires will cost between $600 and $1,000, and their condition will vitally affect the value of the tractor. To obtain good tires with tread appropriate to the year of the tractor can be difficult and even more costly.

Wheels also bear close inspection. Check for corrosion from farm chemicals and tire fluid. Check the wheel-mounting holes for cracks or elongation. Check the wheels for wobble, which could mean a bent rim or axle.

Steel wheels are an even bigger watchout. Steel wheels do not necessarily have to be of the type that came with the tractor but must be appropriate for the vintage of the tractor.

## Steering

Steering wheel free play of about 45 degrees is the limit of acceptability for more or less "modern" tractors. Up to 90 degrees can be tolerated on an A, and maybe 180 degrees on a 15-20 or the like. Determine where the looseness is, however, as it may be an indication of needed expensive repairs.

Grasp the tops of the front wheels and try to move them in and out. Looseness and clunking are an indication of kingpin and/or wheel bearing play. Check the steering wheel itself in the same way to see if all the bearings are sound.

## Engine

As you make these checks, make the engine ready to start; that is, open the fuel shut-off and add oil, fuel, and water as necessary. If the engine is inoperable, do your best to determine why. Is there compression? Is there a spark? Is the fuel getting through? Is the engine "stuck"? A truly stuck engine is a problem but is not insurmountable. Engines can almost always be "unstuck" by pressure—hydraulic pressure. The ultimate way to free an engine is to take it to a machine shop and have the pistons pressed out. Before getting to that point, though, you should try to soak it free by filling the cylinders through the spark plug holes with a penetrating oil (don't put the plugs back in, except very loosely). Periodically, give it a try with the hand crank or with the jacked-up back wheel (which can go back or forth). There are many ways to proceed if you find

A Farmall HV, a Cub, and a Cub Lo-Boy stand side by side. The HV is almost 3ft taller than the Lo-Boy. This set is owned by Case International dealer and Farmall collector Jon Kayser, Dell Rapids, South Dakota.

a stuck engine, but the point here is to correctly evaluate what you are up against and proceed accordingly.

## Electrical

The Ammeter Indication item (on non-magneto systems) is intended to show that the ignition system and switch are functional by observing an indication of "discharge" when the switch is turned on (it may be necessary to rotate the engine with the hand crank until the points close). When checking the lights see if they are genuine International items or aftermarket parts. A four- or five-star restoration must have "the right stuff."

## Clutch/Transmission

It is important to ascertain that the clutch is actually released when the pedal is in the "release" position or the transmission is actually in neutral before attempting to manually start the engine. Failure to do so could result in your being run over!

## Hydraulics

It's best to check the hydraulics with a heavy implement such as a plow or mower deck. The system should be able to raise and hold anything designed for it with ample reserve. With the engine off, the system should not let the implement down for at least ten minutes.

## Road/Field Test

Ideally, you can operate the tractor in a field with an implement such as a plow or mower. You should also take it where you can operate it at top road speed. Try all the gears and the brakes. Operate it long enough for things to get warm. Listen for any unusual sounds as it warms up.

## Summary

Again, remember that the point of these tests is not so much to accept or reject the tractor, but to determine if the price is fair and if you are prepared for the level of work that a particular tractor might require. Some people get their enjoyment from actually doing the work of bringing a class 5 tractor up to a class 1. Others prefer to do the mechanical work and have the painting and finishing done by specialists.

## Buying the Tractor

When considering the purchase of a tractor located at some distance from your base of operations, you should get as much information on its condition as you can before making the trip. You might consider sending the checklist to the owner and asking him to fill it out and return it. Ask him to send along some pictures when he does. Even with precautions, don't be surprised if things are not all that you expected.

It is best to have a price in mind when you first contact the prospective seller, but it is up to the seller to quote his asking price first. The same is true of auctions; have your upper-limit dollar figure firmly in mind before the bidding starts. With the individual seller, you usually start at his price and bargain downward; with the auction, it's the opposite. If you find you are too far apart, tell the seller how you arrived at your figure (based on similar sales, advertisements, or estimated value upon completion of restoration). Then give him your name and phone number on paper and leave. If your facts are convincing, he may come around. You'll not likely cause him to change his price a lot, however, unless he has time to check out your logic.

Don't overlook the opportunity for barter in the transaction. Perhaps you have something to trade or a professional service you can provide to the seller. Also, look for things to be "thrown in" on the deal. For example, the seller may be able to transport the tractor home for you, or you may require that he do some work on it before you take it away.

Once you've struck a deal, you'll be expected to come up with an acceptable form of payment (assuming it wasn't a complete barter deal). If you are close to home, matters are simplified: write a check for the amount, wait for the check to clear, and then pick up your tractor. If waiting is not acceptable, then you'll need cash, a certified check, or traveler's checks. Unless you have already agreed upon a price, the certified check will not likely be for the right amount. Make it out for your initial offer amount, then add to it with cash or traveler's checks to bring the amount up to the agreed upon price. If the amount of the transaction is small, or if the difference is not too great, some sellers may accept a personal check for the difference.

Tractors are unlike automobiles in that they do not have officially registered titles. How do you know, or how can you find out, if the one you are bargaining with really owns the tractor he is trying to sell you? One of the first things you should ask the prospective seller is how long he has had the tractor and where he got it. At that point it's a good idea to ask if he still has the bill of sale. If he doesn't and has not had the tractor long, he should be willing to go back to the previous owner to get one. If he claims to be the original owner of a fifty-year-old tractor and has no purchasing paperwork, you'll have to use your best judgment.

Be sure that when you get your bill of sale, it includes the correct serial number or other identification. If the dollar amount is large or if you are uneasy about the legality of the sale, you might require notarization of the bill. At least you will have some recourse if, after you've completed the restoration, you find out you have to give the tractor back.

Once the money has changed hands and you've gotten the bill of sale, you are the owner. Ordinarily, your homeowner's insurance will be sufficient protection for liabilities during restoration, unless you are restoring tractors as a business. In that case, check with your insurance agent. If you transport the tractor home yourself, your regular truck or trailer insurance should apply to cargo. If the value of your purchase is great, you might be wise to talk to your agent about special coverage for it while in transit and while under restoration.

There are some things you may want to get done on the way home with your tractor. You may want to take it to a place that has an engine degreasing service and have the whole tractor done. Assuming you have already done your best to operate the tractor to determine its condition, you may want to stop at a service station and have the oil, fuel, antifreeze, and tire fluid removed. You can, of course, remove these items in your own shop and then take them to a disposal facility, if you choose, but for most of us, this can be a messy procedure.

## Collection Protection

*Two-Cylinder*, the official publication of Two-Cylinder Clubs, Worldwide, is a magazine for John Deere enthusiasts. A recent issue featured an article by Mr. Craig Beek, John Deere's Manager for Corporate Security. Beek's article provides insights to help keep the antique tractor collector from being victimized by the unscrupulous. It is paraphrased here for the benefit of the International collector.

As more people get into tractor collecting, and as collector tractors become more difficult to find, and especially as values soar, the potential for fraud and theft also increases dramatically. Protect yourself during the buying process by getting and keeping plenty of proof of the transaction. Sometimes deals that sound too good to be true are just that.

Check and record the serial number. If the number is on a plate, examine it to see if it looks newer than the tractor. Does it look as if it has recently been installed? Engine block serial number stampings were often done by hand and can look suspicious. See if you can detect stamp-overs or newly stamped or uneven sized numbers. In most states it is a felony to alter a factory-installed identification number. If an unscrupulous seller sees you are suspicious when you ask for a notarized bill of sale, he's likely to start backing out of the sale.

Serial numbers aren't the only thing to watch out for. Let's say you are buying a low serial W-9 with original steel wheels. It is a good idea to be able to trace the history of the wheels. Did they come with the tractor, or did they come from a tractor that was scrapped out? If the latter is the case, it's best to determine that the scrapped tractor wasn't "chopped" by a thief. In such a case, get notarized documentation as to the legitimate sources of valuable parts.

The best advice to prevent being swindled is to create a paper trail with all important documents notarized. Despite the precautions, if you buy a stolen tractor, you lose. Law enforcement officials and the courts usually hold that a thief can pass no better title than he holds. At least your "black on white" will show you bought the machine in good faith.

Not only can the buyer be swindled by thieves, but he or she can be caught in the cross fire between feuding heirs disputing who has the rights to Grandpa's tractor. The heirs may think it's just a pile of junk. When the sale amounts to thousands of dollars they may then change their minds.

After you have taken possession of the tractor, one of the best things you can do is take photographs or videos of it from every angle. Include the serial number plate or stamping. Also include pictures of valuable parts, such as new tires. You might also want to scribe your driver's license number or Social Security number in inconspicuous places. There is the Iowa System, in which your local sheriff assigns you an Owner Applied Identification Number (OAN) based on your state, county, and name. The number is to be die-stamped somewhere on the tractor. When the tractor is sold, the new owner die-stamps his or her number below yours. If your tractor is stolen, you will want all the data and identification possible to give to the police! The investigating officer can enter the data in the FBI's National Crime Information Center (NCIC) computer, which serves as a link between law enforcement agencies.

Again, make sure your insurance company knows about the tractor, especially if it is other than run-of-the-mill. It should be handled just like any other valuable antique.

Finally, there is the prospect of taking your completed gem to a show. You put it in the line with the rest and then walk off to see the others. What about that battery box cover or radiator cap that you struggled for so long to find? Do you remove such items and put them in your locked pickup? At the present time, at least, that's going a little too far. Just be sure that your "numbers" are stamped or scribed on the inside. Leaving the tractor for the night is another matter, however. It's good to have cheap replacement parts to use in such a situation. If you have something really valuable, such as a five-star, class 1 ID-40, you should have an enclosed trailer with a good hitch lock.

Should all this put a damper on your desire to get into collecting? Not at all. Just exercise proper precautions. On the whole, antique tractor people are by nature the absolute nicest people you are likely to run across, and the unscrupulous are very few and far between.

# Model, Serial Number, and Production Year Summary

This list will help you determine a tractor's year model by listing the beginning serial number for the production year.

| Model | Beginning Serial No. | Year |
|---|---|---|
| 15-30 | TG112 | 1921 |
| | TG311 | 1922 |
| | TG1661 | 1923 |
| | TG6547 | 1924 |
| | TG13868 | 1925 |
| | TG26846 | 1926 |
| | TG48647 | 1927 |
| | TG64401 | 1928 |

| Model | Beginning Serial No. | Year |
|---|---|---|
| 22-36 | TG99926 | 1929 |
| | TG128237 | 1930 |
| | TG150128 | 1931 |
| | TG154508 | 1932 |
| | TG156213 | 1933 |
| | TG156301 | 1934 |

| Model | Beginning Serial No. | Year |
|---|---|---|
| 10-20 | KC501 | 1923 |
| | KC7641 | 1924 |
| | KC18869 | 1925 |
| | KC37728 | 1926 |
| | KC62824 | 1927 |
| | KC89470 | 1928 |
| | KC119823 | 1929 |
| | KC159111 | 1930 |
| | KC191486 | 1931 |
| | KC201013 | 1932 |
| | KC204239 | 1934* |
| | KC206179 | 1935 |
| | KC207275 | 1936 |
| | KC210235 | 1937 |
| | KC212425 | 1938 |
| | KC214886 | 1939 |

KC: regular tread
* After 1934, the suffix NT was added to indicate narrow tread

| Model | Beginning Serial No. | Year |
|---|---|---|
| 10-20 | NC501 | 1926 |
| | NC649 | 1927 |
| | NC832 | 1928 |
| | NC1155 | 1929 |
| | NC1543 | 1930 |
| | NC1750 | 1931 |
| | NC1833 | 1932 |
| | NC1912 | 1933 |
| | NC1952 | 1934 |

NC: narrow tread

| Model | Beginning Serial No. | Year |
|---|---|---|
| Regular | QC501 | 1924 |
| | QC701 | 1925 |
| | QC1539 | 1926 |
| | T1569 | 1927 |
| | T15471 | 1928 |
| | T40370 | 1929 |

| Model | Beginning Serial No. | Year |
|---|---|---|
|  | T75691 | 1930 |
|  | T117784 | 1931 |
|  | T131872 | 1932 |

| Model | Beginning Serial No. | Year |
|---|---|---|
| F-30 | FB501 | 1931 |
|  | FB1184 | 1932 |
|  | FB4305 | 1933 |
|  | FB5526 | 1934 |
|  | FB7032 | 1935 |
|  | FB10407 | 1936 |
|  | FB18684 | 1937 |
|  | FB27186 | 1938 |
|  | FB29007 | 1939 |

| Model | Beginning Serial No. | Year |
|---|---|---|
| F 20 | FA/TA501 | 1932 |
|  | FA/TA3001 | 1933 |
|  | TA135000 (to TA135661) | 1934 |
|  | TA6382 | 1935 |
|  | TA32716 | 1936 |
|  | TA68749 | 1937 |
|  | TA105597 | 1938 |
|  | TA130865 (to TA134999) | 1939 |
|  | TA135700 | 1939 |

| Model | Beginning Serial No. | Year |
|---|---|---|
| F-12 | FS501 | 1932 |
|  | FS526 | 1933 |
|  | FS4881 | 1934 |
|  | FS17411 | 1935 |
|  | FS48660 | 1936 |
|  | FS81837 | 1937 |
|  | FS117518 | 1938 |

| Model | Beginning Serial No. | Year |
|---|---|---|
| F-14 | FS124000 | 1938 |
|  | FS139607 | 1939 |

| Model | Beginning Serial No. | Year |
|---|---|---|
| Cub | FCUB501 | 1947 |
|  | FCUB11348 | 1948 |

| Model | Beginning Serial No. | Year |
|---|---|---|
|  | FCUB57831 | 1949 |
|  | FCUB99536 | 1950 |
|  | FCUB121454 | 1951 |
|  | FCUB144455 | 1952 |
|  | FCUB162284 | 1953 |
|  | FCUB179412 | 1954 |
|  | FCUB186441 | 1955 |
|  | FCUB193658 | 1956 |
|  | FCUB198231 | 1957 |

| Model | Beginning Serial No. | Year |
|---|---|---|
| A and B | 501 | 1939 |
|  | 6744 | 1940 |
|  | 41500 | 1941 |
|  | 80739 | 1942 |
|  | none | 1943 |
|  | 96390 | 1944 |
|  | 113218 | 1945 |
|  | 146700 | 1946 |
|  | 1982964 | 1947 |

A: FAA; AV: FAAV; B: FAB; BN: FABN

| Model | Beginning Serial No. | Year |
|---|---|---|
| Super A | 25001 | 1947 |
|  | 250082 | 1948 |
|  | 268196 | 1949 |
|  | 281569 | 1950 |
|  | 300126 | 1951 |
|  | 324470 | 1952 |
|  | 336880 | 1953 |
|  | 353348 | 1954 |

Super A: SA

| Model | Beginning Serial No. | Year |
|---|---|---|
| C | FC501 | 1948 |
|  | FC22524 | 1949 |
|  | FC47010 | 1950 |
|  | FC71880 | 1951 |

| Model | Beginning Serial No. | Year |
|---|---|---|
| Super C | FSC100001 | 1951 |
|  | FSC131157 | 1952 |
|  | FSC159130 | 1953 |
|  | FSC187788 | 1954 |

| Model | Beginning Serial No. | Year |
|---|---|---|
| H | 501 | 1939 |
| | 10653 | 1940 |
| | 52387 | 1941 |
| | 93237 | 1942 |
| | 12250 | 1943 |
| | 15051 | 1944 |
| | 186123 | 1945 |
| | 214820 | 1946 |
| | 241143 | 1947 |
| | 268991 | 1948 |
| | 300876 | 1949 |
| | 327975 | 1950 |
| | 351923 | 1951 |
| | 375861 | 1952 |
| | 390500 | 1953 |

H: FBH; HV: FBHV

| Model | Beginning Serial No. | Year |
|---|---|---|
| Super H | 501 | 1953 |
| | 22202 | 1954 |

F: SH, SHV

| Model | Beginning Serial No. | Year |
|---|---|---|
| M | 501 | 1939 |
| | 7240 | 1940 |
| | 25371 | 1941 |
| | 50988 | 1942 |
| | 60011 | 1943 |
| | 67424 | 1944 |
| | 88085 | 1945 |
| | 105564 | 1946 |
| | 122823 | 1947 |
| | 151708 | 1948 |
| | 180514 | 1949 |
| | 213579 | 1950 |
| | 247518 | 1951 |
| | 290923 | 1952 |

M: FBK; MV: FBKV; MD: FDBK; MDV: FDBKV

| Model | Beginning Serial No. | Year |
|---|---|---|
| Super M | 501 | 1952 |
| | 12516 | 1953 |
| | 51977 | 1954 |

F: SM; M: TA

| Model | Beginning Serial No. | Year |
|---|---|---|
| Super M | TA60001 | 1954 |

| Model | Beginning Serial No. | Year |
|---|---|---|
| McCormick W-4 | 501 | 1940 |
| | 943 | |
| | 4056 | |
| | 5693 | |
| | 7593 | |
| | 11171 | |
| | 13934 | |
| | 16022 | |
| | 18880 | |
| | 21912 | |
| | 22470 | |
| | 28167 | |
| | 31214 | |
| | 33069 | |

| Model | Beginning Serial No. | Year |
|---|---|---|
| Super W-4 | 501 | 1953 |
| | 2668 | 1954 |

| Model | Beginning Serial No. | Year |
|---|---|---|
| McCormick W-6 | 501 | 1940 |
| | 1225 | 1941 |
| | 3718 | 1942 |
| | 5057 | 1943 |
| | 6313 | 1944 |
| | 9496 | 1945 |
| | 14153 | 1946 |
| | 17792 | 1947 |
| | 22981 | 1948 |
| | 28704 | 1949 |
| | 33698 | 1950 |
| | 38518 | 1951 |
| | 44318 | 1952 |
| | 45274 | 1953 |

| Model | Beginning Serial No. | Year |
|---|---|---|
| Super W-6 | 501 | 1952 |
| | 2908 | 1953 |
| | 8997 | 1954 |

| Model | Beginning Serial No. | Year |
|---|---|---|
| Super W-6 | TA 10001 | 1954 |

| Model | Beginning Serial No. | Year |
|---|---|---|
| McCormick W-9 | 501 | 1940 |
| | 578 | 1941 |
| | 2993 | 1942 |
| | 3651 | 1943 |
| | 5394 | 1944 |
| | 11459 | 1945 |
| | 17289 | 1946 |
| | 22714 | 1947 |
| | 29207 | 1948 |
| | 36159 | 1949 |
| | 45551 | 1950 |
| | 51739 | 1951 |
| | 59407 | 1952 |
| | 64014 | 1953 |

| Model | Beginning Serial No. | Year |
|---|---|---|
| Super WD-9 | 501 | 1953 |
| | 1935 | 1954 |
| | 5238 | 1955 |
| | 6864 | 1956 |

| Model | Beginning Serial No. | Year |
|---|---|---|
| McCormick WR-9S | 501 | 1953 |
| | 550 | 1954 |
| | 722 | 1955 |
| | 735 | 1956 |

| Model | Beginning Serial No. | Year |
|---|---|---|
| F-100 | 501 | 1954 |
| | 1720 | 1955 |
| | 12895 | 1956 |

| Model | Beginning Serial No. | Year |
|---|---|---|
| I-100 | 501 | 1954 |
| | 504 | 1955 |
| | 575 | 1956 |

| Model | Beginning Serial No. | Year |
|---|---|---|
| F-200 | 501 | 1954 |
| | 1032 | 1955 |
| | 10904 | 1956 |

| Model | Beginning Serial No. | Year |
|---|---|---|
| F-300 | 01 | 1954 |
| | 1779 | 1955 |
| | 23224 | 1956 |

| Model | Beginning Serial No. | Year |
|---|---|---|
| I-300 | 501 | 1955 |
| | 20219 | 1956 |

| Model | Beginning Serial No. | Year |
|---|---|---|
| F-400 | 501 | 1954 |
| | 2588 | 1955 |
| | 29065 | 1956 |

| Model | Beginning Serial No. | Year |
|---|---|---|
| I-400 | 501 | 1955 |
| | 2187 | 1956 |

| Model | Beginning Serial No. | Year |
|---|---|---|
| F-130 | 501 | 1956 |
| | 1120 | 1957 |
| | 8363 | 1958 |

| Model | Beginning Serial No. | Year |
|---|---|---|
| F-230 | 501 | 1956 |
| | 815 | 1957 |
| | 6827 | 1958 |

| Model | Beginning Serial No. | Year |
|---|---|---|
| I-330 | 501 | 1957 |
| | 1488 | 1958 |

| Model | Beginning Serial No. | Year |
|---|---|---|
| F and I-140 | 501 | 1958 |
| | 2011 | 1959 |
| | 8082 | 1960 |
| | 11168 | 1961 |
| | 16637 | 1962 |
| | 21181 | 1963 |
| | 24716 | 1964 |
| | 27964 | 1965 |
| | 30775 | 1966 |
| | 34325 | 1967 |

| Model | Beginning Serial No. | Year |
|---|---|---|
| 36927 | 1968 | |
| | 39514 | 1969 |
| | 37767 | 1970 |
| | 44424 | 1971 |
| | 46605 | 1972 |
| | 48507 | 1973 |
| | 50720 | 1974 |
| | 54723 | 1975 |

| Model | Beginning Serial No. | Year |
|---|---|---|
| F-240 | 501 | 1958 |
| | 1777 | 1959 |
| | 3415 | 1960 |
| | 3889 | 1961 |

| Model | Beginning Serial No. | Year |
|---|---|---|
| I-240 | 501 | 1958 |
| | 4835 | 1959 |
| | 8628 | 1960 |
| | 10079 | 1961 |
| | 10727 | 1962 |

| Model | Beginning Serial No. | Year |
|---|---|---|
| F-340 | 501 | 1958 |
| | 2723 | 1959 |
| | 5411 | 1960 |
| | 6642 | 1961 |
| | 7626 | 1962 |
| | 7699 | 1963 |

| Model | Beginning Serial No. | Year |
|---|---|---|
| I-340 | 501 | 1958 |
| | 2467 | 1959 |
| | 5741 | 1960 |
| | 6642 | 1961 |
| | 11141 | 1962 |
| | 12032 | 1963 |

| Model | Beginning Serial No. | Year |
|---|---|---|
| F-350 | 501 | 1956 |
| | 1004 | 1957 |
| | 14175 | 1958 |

| Model | Beginning Serial No. | Year |
|---|---|---|
| F-450 | 501 | 1956 |
| | 1734 | 1957 |
| | 21871 | 1958 |

| Model | Beginning Serial No. | Year |
|---|---|---|
| I-450 | 501 | 1956 |
| | 568 | 1957 |
| | 1661 | 1959 |

| Model | Beginning Serial No. | Year |
|---|---|---|
| F-460 | 501 | 1958 |
| | 4766 | 1959 |
| | 16900 | 1960 |
| | 22622 | 1961 |
| | 28029 | 1962 |
| | 31522 | 1963 |

| Model | Beginning Serial No. | Year |
|---|---|---|
| I-460 | 501 | 1958 |
| | 2711 | 1959 |
| | 6883 | 1960 |
| | 9420 | 1961 |
| | 11619 | 1962 |
| | 11898 | 1963 |

| Model | Beginning Serial No. | Year |
|---|---|---|
| F-560 | 501 | 1958 |
| | 7341 | 1959 |
| | 26914 | 1960 |
| | 36125 | 1961 |
| | 47798 | 1962 |
| | 60278 | 1963 |

| Model | Beginning Serial No. | Year |
|---|---|---|
| I-560 | 501 | 1958 |
| | 1210 | 1959 |
| | 3103 | 1960 |
| | 4032 | 1961 |
| | 4944 | 1962 |
| | 5598 | 1963 |

| Model | Beginning Serial No. | Year | Model | Beginning Serial No. | Year |
|-------|------------|------|-------|------------|------|
| I-600 | 501 | 1956 | I-660 | 501 | 1959 |
|       |            |      |       | 3398 | 1960 |
| Model | Beginning Serial No. | Year |   | 4259 | 1961 |
| I-650 | 501 | 1956 |   | 5853 | 1962 |
|       | 688 | 1957 |   | 6995 | 1963 |
|       | 11659 | 1958 |   |      |      |

*Appendix 2*

# International Tractor Specifications

| Model | Bore/Stroke | Cyl. | Rated RPM | Forward Speeds | Basic Weight | Rear Tire Size |
|-------|-------------|------|-----------|----------------|--------------|----------------|
| 15-30 | 4.50x6.00 | 4 | 1,000 | 3 | 6,000 | |
| 15-30 | 4.75x6.00 | 4 | 1,050 | 3 | 7,486 | |
| 10-20 | 4.25x5.00 | 4 | 1,100 | 3 | 4,010 | |
| WK-40 | 3.75x4.5 | 6 | 1,750 | 3 | 5,600 | |
| Regular | 3.75x5.00 | 4 | 1,200 | 3 | 4,100 | 40x6 |
| F-30 | 4.25x5.00 | 4 | 1,150 | 3 | 5,990 | 42x12 |
| F-20 | 3.75x5.00 | 4 | 1,200 | 4 | 4,545 | 40x6 |
| F-12 | 3.00x4.00 | 4 | 1,400 | 3 | 3,280 | 54x6 |
| F-14 | 3.00x4.00 | 4 | 1,650 | 3 | 3,820 | 40x9 |
| Cub | 2.62x2.75 | 4 | 1,600 | 3 | 1,540 | 8x24 |
| Cub | 2.62x2.75 | 4 | 1,800 | 3 | 1,550 | 8x24 |
| A | 3.00x4.00 | 4 | 1,400 | 4 | 2,014 | 8x24 |

| Model | Bore/Stroke | Cyl. | Rated RPM | Forward Speeds | Basic Weight | Rear Tire Size |
|---|---|---|---|---|---|---|
| B | | | 1,400 | | 2,150 | 9x24 |
| Super A | | | 1,650 | | 2,363 | |
| C | 3.00x4.00 | 4 | 1,650 | 4 | 2,845 | 9x36 |
| Super C | 3.13x4.00 | 4 | 1,650 | 4 | 3,209 | 10x36 |
| H | 3.38x4.25 | 4 | 1,650 | 5 | 3,694 | 10x36 |
| Super H | 3.50x4.25 | | 1,650 | 5 | 4,389 | 11x38 |
| M | .88x5.25 | 4 | 1,450 | 5 | 4,858 | 11x38 |
| MD | 3.88x5.25 | | 1,450 | 5 | 5,300 | 12x38 |
| Super M | 4.00x5.25 | | 1,450 | 5 | 5,600 | 13x38 |
| SuperMD | 4.00x5.25 | | 1,450 | 5 | 6,034 | 13x38 |
| 100 | 3.13x4.00 | 4 | 1,400 | 4 | 3,038 | 11x24 |
| 130 | 3.13x4.00 | 4 | 1,400 | 4 | 3,050 | 11x24 |
| 200 | 3.13x4.00 | 4 | 1,650 | 4 | 3,541 | 10x36 |
| 230 | 3.13x4.00 | 4 | 1,800 | 4 | 3,550 | 11x36 |
| 300 | .56x4.25 | 4 | 1,750 | 5 | 4,800 | 11x38 |
| 330 | 3.25x4.06 | 4 | 2,000 | 5 | 4,360 | 12x28 |
| 350D | 3.75x4.38 | 4 | 1,750 | 5 | 5,000 | 13x38 |
| 400 | 4.00x5.25 | 4 | 1,450 | 5 | 6,519 | 11x38 |
| 450 | 4.13x5.25 | 4 | 1,450 | 5 | 6,520 | 11x38 |
| 460D | 3.69x3.69 | 6 | 1,800 | 5 | 6,500 | 14x38 |
| 560 | 3.56x4.39 | 6 | 1,800 | 5 | 6,600 | 16x38 |
| 560D | 3.69x4.39 | 6 | 1,800 | 5 | 6,800 | 16x38 |
| 650 | 4.50x5.5 | 4 | 1,500 | 5 | 9,000 | 18x26 |
| 660D | 3.69x4.39 | 6 | 2,400 | 5 | 10,000 | 18x26 |

# Nebraska Tractor Test Summary

Tractor sales peaked in 1920 at about 200,000 units. The war boom was over, but manufacturers did not know to adjust their output. Sales in 1921 amounted to only 35,000 tractors and the industry was devastated. Some of the drop in sales was due to falling crop prices, but much was due to the fact that farmers were becoming increasingly wary of unscrupulous tractor makers.

Defective tractors, overly enthusiastic advertising, and "paper" tractor companies had caused the farmers to clamor for consumer protection even before the boom war years. In 1915, *Power Farming* magazine had called for the standardization of horsepower and capacity ratings, but the industry did not respond. The magazine continued to editorialize for a national rating system, saying that the states would act if the federal government failed, and this would result in a hodgepodge of requirements.

The federal government did not react, so in early 1919, a Nebraska legislator, Wilmot F. Crozier, introduced a bill that would require all tractors sold in Nebraska to be submitted for testing. Crozier was also a farmer who had had poor experience with oversold and underdesigned tractors. Crozier's bill provided for the testing to be done by the University of Nebraska. Another aspect of the bill was that manufacturers would be required to keep an adequate stock of spare parts in the state.

The Nebraska Tractor Test Law went into effect on July 15, 1919. The Nebraska program was so comprehensive that other states abandoned their own plans and relied on Nebraska's results, as indeed did much of the world.

Testing began in the fall of 1919, but an early snowfall interrupted the activities until the spring of 1920. The first tractor to successfully qualify for sale in Nebraska under the new law was the Waterloo Boy Model N. Since that time, the Nebraska Tractor Tests have been the common yardstick by which tractor performance is measured.

The results of International Harvester tractor tests are summarized in the following chart.

| Model | Test Number | Fuel | Max. HP Belt/PTO | Max. HP Drawbar | Max. Pull | Fuel Cons. | Weight | Wheels | Year |
|-------|-------------|------|------------------|-----------------|-----------|-----------|--------|--------|------|
| 15-30 | 84 | K | 32.8 | 19.9 | 2,790 | 9.78 | 6,000 | S | 1922 |
| 10-20 | 95 | K | 24.9 | 15.5 | 2,640 | 10.2 | 4,010 | S | 1923 |
| Regular | 117 | K | 20.1 | 12.7 | 2,727 | 9.39 | 4,100 | S | 1925 |
| 15-30 | 156 | K | 40.6 | 30.0 | 3,912 | 9.99 | 7,486 | S | 1929 |

| Model | Test Number | Fuel | Max. HP Belt/PTO | Max. HP Drawbar | Max. Pull | Fuel Cons. | Weight | Wheels | Year |
|---|---|---|---|---|---|---|---|---|---|
| F-30 | 198 | K | 32.8 | 24.6 | 4,157 | 9.61 | 5,990 | S | 1931 |
| F-20 | 221 | K | 23.1 | 15.4 | 2,334 | 10.4 | 4,545 | S | 1934 |
| W-12 | 231 | G | 17.7 | 13.5 | 2,140 | 10.1 | 3,360 | S | 1934 |
| F-20 | 264 | Dis. | 26.8 | 18.8 | 2,799 | 9.82 | 4,400 | S | 1936 |
| F-20 | 276 | Dis. | 26.7 | 19.6 | 2,927 | 10.5 | 4,310 | S | 1936 |
| F-12 | 212 | G | 16.2 | 10.1 | 1,172 | 9.54 | 3,280 | S | 1933 |
| F-12 | 220 | K | 14.6 | 11.8 | 1,814 | 10.0 | 3,240 | S | 1933 |
| F-14 | 297 | Dis. | 17.0 | 13.2 | 2,369 | 10.9 | 4,900 | R | 1938 |
| Cub | 386 | G | 9.23 | 8.34 | 1,596 | 10.9 | 1,539 | R | 1947 |
| Cub | 575 | G | 10.4 | 9.63 | 1,605 | 9.38 | 2,393 | R | 1956 |
| A | 329 | G | 16.8 | 12.3 | 2,387 | 12.0 | 3,570 | R | 1939 |
| A | 330 | Dis. | 16.5 | 15.2 | 2,360 | 11.9 | 3,500 | R | 1939 |
| B | 331 | G | 16.8 | 12.1 | 2,377 | 11.9 | 3,740 | R | 1939 |
| B | 332 | Dis. | 15.4 | 12.0 | 2,463 | 11.8 | 3,700 | R | 1939 |
| C | 395 | G | 19.9 | 15.9 | 2,902 | 11.2 | 4,409 | R | 1948 |
| Super C | 458 | G | 23.7 | 20.7 | N/A | 10.8 | 5,041 | R | 1951 |
| H | 333 | G | 24.3 | 19.8 | 3,603 | 11.7 | 5,550 | R | 1939 |
| H | 334 | Dis. | 22.1 | 19.4 | 3,169 | 11.8 | 5,550 | R | 1939 |
| Super W4 | 491 | G | 31.5 | 6.3 | 4,501 | 11.7 | 6,913 | R | 1953 |
| Super H | 492 | G | 31.3 | 26.0 | 4,178 | 11.7 | 6,713 | R | 1953 |
| M | 327 | Dis. | 34.2 | 25.5 | 4,365 | 12.5 | 6,770 | R | 1939 |
| M | 328 | G | 36.1 | 24.5 | 4,233 | 12.2 | 6,770 | R | 1939 |
| MD | 368 | D | 35.0 | N/A | 4,541 | 14.6 | 7,570 | R | 1941 |
| SuperM | 475 | G | 43.9 | 37.1 | 5,676 | 12.0 | 8,929 | R | 1952 |
| SuperM | 484 | LPG | 45.7 | 39.5 | 6,115 | 8.76 | 9,145 | R | 1952 |
| SuperMD | 477 | D | 46.7 | 37.7 | 5,772 | 13.9 | 9,338 | R | 1952 |
| SuperWD9 | 518 | D | 65.2 | 46.2 | 8,416 | 14.6 | 12,795 | R | 1954 |
| 100 | 537 | G | 18.3 | 15.8 | 2,503 | 10.6 | 4,338 | R | 1955 |
| 200 | 536 | G | 24.1 | 20.9 | 3,166 | 10.8 | 5,331 | R | 1955 |
| 240U | 668 | G | 28.6 | 21.9 | 4,384 | 12.2 | 5,745 | R | 1958 |
| 300 | 538 | G | 40.0 | 30.0 | 4,852 | 11.8 | 8,257 | R | 1955 |
| 350U | 615 | G | 41.1 | 31.2 | 6,029 | 11.6 | 7,695 | R | 1957 |
| 400 | 532 | G | 50.8 | 45.3 | 6,508 | 12.1 | 9,669 | R | 1955 |
| 400 | 534 | D | 46.7 | 41.6 | 6,415 | 13.9 | 9,700 | R | 1955 |
| 400 | 571 | LPG | 52.4 | 46.7 | 6,374 | 9.78 | 9,900 | R | 1956 |
| 450 | 612 | G | 51.6 | N/A | 7,318 | 12.5 | 8,905 | R | 1957 |
| 460U | 674 | G | 46.7 | N/A | 6,485 | 12.2 | 8,295 | R | 1958 |
| 560 | 669 | D | 58.5 | N/A | 7,347 | 14.8 | 9,460 | R | 1958 |
| 650 | 618 | G | 59.0 | 50.0 | 8,564 | 11.6 | 12,605 | R | 1957 |
| 660D | 715 | D | 78.8 | 64.4 | N/A | 14.2 | 15,255 | R | 1959 |

## Notes on Nebraska Tractor Tests:

**Fuel:** K: Kerosene; Dis.: Distillate; D: Diesel; LPG: Liquefied Petroleum Gas, or Propane.

**Belt/PTO HP:** This is Test C horsepower, maximum attainable at the PTO or belt pulley. If the generator, hydraulic pump, etc., were not standard equipment, they were removed for these tests. Note that Nebraska test data published during this period are not corrected to standard atmospheric conditions.

**Drawbar HP:** Taken from Test G data, it is based on maximum drawbar pull and speed. The difference between this and PTO HP is due to slippage, and to the power required to move the tractor itself. The heavier the tractor, the less the slippage, but the more power required to move the tractor. Factory engineers looked for the ideal compromise.

**Max. Pull:** Test G. The pull used for calculating drawbar HP.

**Fuel Cons.:** The rate of fuel consumption in horsepower hours per gallon taken from Test C conditions. The higher the number, the better.

**Pull:** In pounds.

**Weight:** The weight of the tractor plus ballast in pounds. Ballast was often added for Test G and other heavy pulling tests, and then removed for other tests to improve performance.

**Wheels:** Steel or Rubber.

# Notes and Recommended Reading

## Books

The following books offer essential background on the International Harvester Company's origins and history, and about the tractors and equipment of the times. These make good reading and library additions for any Farmall buff. Most are available from Motorbooks International Publishers & Wholesalers, P.O. Box 2, 729 Prospect Avenue, Osceola, Wisconsin 54020 USA.

*The Agricultural Tractor 1855-1950*, by R.B. Gray, Society of Agricultural Engineers; an outstanding and complete photo history of the origin and development of the tractor.

*The American Farm Tractor*, by Randy Leffingwell, Motorbooks International; a full-color hardback history of all the great American tractor makes.

*The Century of the Reaper*, by Cyrus McCormick III, Houghton Mifflin Company; a firsthand account of the Harvester and Tractor Wars by the grandson of the inventor. Several of McCormick's vignettes are included verbatim to give a flavor of the times.

*A Corporate Tragedy*, by Barbara Marsh, Doubleday and Company; an intriguing account of the development of International Harvester Company and the ultimate sale of its farm equipment business to Tenneco in 1984. Much scholarly research and journalistic writing are evinced in this work; it's a "must read" for Farmall fans.

*The Development of American Agriculture*, by Willard W. Cochrane, University of Minnesota Press; an analytical history.

*Farm Tractors 1926-1956*, Randy Stephens, Editor, Intertec Publishing; a compilation of pages from *The Cooperative Tractor Catalog* and the *Red Tractor Book*.

*Fordson, Farmall and Poppin' Johnny*, by Robert C. Williams, University of Illinois Press; a history of the farm tractor and its impact on America.

*Ford Tractors*, by Robert N. Pripps and Andrew Morland, Motorbooks International; a full-color history of the Fordson, Ford-Ferguson, Ferguson, and Ford tractors, covering the influence these historic tractors had on the state of the art of tractor design.

*Ford and Fordson Tractors*, by Michael Williams, Blandford Press; a history of Henry Ford and his tractors, concentrating on the Fordson.

*Harvest Triumphant*, by Merrill Denison, WM. Collins Sons & Company, LTD; the story of human achievement in the development of agricultural tools, especially in Canada, and the rise to prominence of Massey Harris Ferguson (now known as the Verity Corporation). Rich in the romance of farm life of the last century and covering the early days of the Industrial Revolution.

*How to Restore Your Farm Tractor*, by Robert N. Pripps, Motorbooks International;

follows two tractors through professional restoration, one a 1939 Farmall A. Includes tips and techniques, commentary, and photos.

*International Harvester Tractors*, by Henry Rasmussen, Motorbooks International; a photo essay on "Reliable Red."

*Threshers*, by Robert N. Pripps and Andrew Morland, Motorbooks International; a color history of grain harvesting and threshing featuring photos and descriptions of many of the big threshers in operation.

*The Yearbook of Agriculture-1960*, U.S. Department of Agriculture.

*150 Years of International Harvester*, by C.H. Wendel, Crestline Publishing; a complete photo-documented product history of International Harvester.

## Helpful People and Organizations

Roger Grozinger of Rusch Equipment Company, Freeport, Illinois, supplied serial number details and other help about Farmalls. Rusch Equipment is a Case International dealer.

## Other Interesting Publications

For a directory of engine and threshing shows, Stemgas Publishing Company issues an annual directory. Their address is: P.O. Box 328 Lancaster, Pennsylvania 17603, 717-392-0733. It lists shows in virtually every area of the country. Stemgas also publishes the enthusiasts' magazines, *Gas Engine Magazine* and *Iron-men Album*.

## Clubs and Newsletters

Newsletters providing a wealth of information and lore about individual brands of antique farm tractors and equipment have been on the scene for some time. More are springing up each year, so the following list is far from complete.

| Name | Editor | Address |
| --- | --- | --- |
| *Antique Power* | Patrick Ertel | P.O. Box 838 Yellow Springs, OH 45387 |
| *Green Magazine* John Deere | Richard Hain | R.R. 1, Bee, NE 68314 |
| *IH Collectors* | | RR 2, Box 286 Winamac, IN 46996 |
| *M-M Corresponder* Minn-Moline | Roger Mohr | Rt. 1, Box 153, Vail, IA 51465 |
| *9N-2N-8N Newsletter* Ford | G.W. Rinaldi | P.O. Box 235 Chelsea, VT 05038-0235 |
| *Old Abe's News* Case | David T. Erb | Rt. 2, Box 2427, Vinton, OH 45686 |
| *Old Allis News* Allis-Chalmers | Nan Jones | 10925 Love Rd., Belleview, MI 49021 |
| *Oliver Collector's News* | Dennis Gerszewski | Rt. 1, Manvel, ND 58256-0044 |
| *Prairie Gold Rush* Minn.-Moline | R. Baumgartner | Rt. 1, Walnut, IL 61376 |
| *Red Power* International Harvester | Daryl Miller | Box 277 Battle Creek, IA 51006 |
| *Wild Harvest* Massey-Harris-Ferguson | Keith Oltrogge | 1010 S. Powell, Box 529, Denver, IA 50622 |

# Index